Accountability is Expected

Trust-first ownership with clear expectations, quick check-ins, fair consequences, and repair. PLUS scripts to end excuses and drive follow-through.

George Munson

GL Digital Publishing LLC

Contents

Introduction

You look at the clock and realize another hour has passed. Emails keep coming in. Your to-do list is full of unfinished tasks. You told yourself you'd finish that project today, but instead, you find yourself scrolling and stressed. The pressure is real. People are counting on you, your team, your boss, maybe even your family. Still, it feels like you're stuck in a loop: you set a goal, make a plan, start strong, then lose momentum. Frustration grows, guilt sets in, and the cycle starts over.

I understand this feeling. I tried every productivity tip and planner, hoping for an easy fix. I depended on willpower to get through tough days. But when stress came, my plans fell apart. I often took on too much and didn't deliver. I'd tell myself I'd do better next time. Sometimes I did, but more often, I didn't.

You're not lazy or broken. You're not alone. I've helped adults, leaders, managers, parents, and many others overcome procrastination and build accountability. I've worked with people facing big decisions. I've seen people feel overwhelmed by constant demands. Life changes when someone matches their actions with values. Not just when things are easy, but also when life is tough.

If you stick with this book, you'll learn how to get things done with habits and systems that last. You'll stay consistent even when life is unpredictable and motivate yourself when willpower fades. You'll create lasting accountability.

This book isn't about quick fixes or empty motivation. Every idea comes from research, experience, and real-world testing. I've used psychology, behavioral science, and the stories of high achievers and everyday people. You won't just get theory here. You'll get tools, frameworks, and routines you can start using right away.

Let's talk about real struggles. Maybe you've set big goals, but they faded away. Maybe you promised your family you'd be more present, but work pulls you back. Maybe you want to be a respected leader, but you worry you'll fall short. Maybe you're tired of guilt and excuses. Maybe you feel like life happens to you. If this sounds familiar, you're in the right place.

You might feel skeptical. Maybe you've tried books, systems, or apps; some helped, but nothing lasted. I'm here to walk with you, challenge you, and share what really works. Perfection isn't the goal, but progress and perseverance are.

What sets this book apart is its practical, step-by-step approach, designed for busy, ambitious, and sometimes overwhelmed people like you. Instead of relying on theory or willpower alone, you'll find specific systems and tools that deliver lasting accountability. These frameworks blend research-driven strategies with actionable routines, helping you achieve self-discipline and track real progress, no matter how demanding life gets.

This book is for you if you want to:

- Track your habits and actually stick with them.

- Motivate yourself when willpower runs out.

- Balance self-discipline with understanding for others.

- Build habits that match your core values.

- Become a role model of responsibility and growth for your family, team, or community.

This book isn't for you if you want shortcuts or "hacks" that avoid real effort. It's also not for you if you want to hear that everything will be easy. Change is hard, and building accountability takes work. But it's possible, and it's worth it.

Here's what you can expect. We won't focus only on motivation. You'll learn why willpower often lets us down. You'll read real stories from people who made accountability a daily habit. You'll learn how to set up systems, trackers, routines, and partnerships that help you stay honest and thrive under stress. We'll cover ways to stay consistent, even when life is unpredictable. You'll find practical checklists, templates, and questions to guide you. Each section ends with clear, simple steps you can use right away.

I wrote this book because I believe accountability is the foundation of a full life. It's not about being hard on yourself or following strict rules. It's about learning to trust yourself, owning your choices, and showing up for what matters. Let your actions reflect your values. Look back and know you gave your best. Not just when things were easy, but when it really counted.

Here's my invitation: let's stop waiting for the perfect time or plan. Let's move from making excuses to taking action together. As you read, I promise you'll gain practical tools, the courage to start, and clarity to sustain momentum. You'll learn how to build a life that's true to you, and you'll see real progress, even in difficult times. The journey starts now, and you don't have to do it alone.

Chapter One

Rethinking Accountability Beyond Blame and Buzzwords

Tension peaks after a missed deadline. Rather than an honest conversation, there's a flurry of unclear emails and whispered side chats. An accountability meeting is called. While blame hangs in the air, the real chance for growth appears. Some defend, excuse, or withdraw in silence. Yet trust can be rebuilt and improvement made. Does accountability always mean blame, or can it guide positive change?

This story is familiar. I once thought accountability meant calling people out or enforcing rules. At first, I believed strict measures or systems would get results, but pressure pushed people away. Teams stopped speaking up, and even holding myself accountable felt like punishment rather than support. Now, this chapter is about positive change.

Why Accountability Gets a Bad Rap and How to Flip the Script

Most people feel uneasy about accountability. However, what if we viewed it differently? Instead of dreading reviews or fearing blame, imagine accountability as support and an opportunity to improve together. In this sense, being "held accountable" can mean growth rather than blame.

Leaders feel this too. Accountability often means endless checklists. Meetings skip the real reasons things went wrong. Instead, they focus more on avoiding blame than solving problems.

This mindset lingers, but it can change. When people feel supported, they speak up and share. As a result, teams have honest conversations. Then, frustration lifts, deadlines are met, and problems are solved. Trust grows, people help each other, and progress accelerates as everyone works together.

These misunderstandings do more than make us uneasy; they hurt results. When people fear blame, they hide problems until they grow out of control. Feedback stops; no one wants conflict. Even in families or volunteer groups, people avoid saying why things fall through, so nothing improves. The cycle repeats, underscoring why a new accountability approach is so needed.

Accountability isn't about watching or punishing. It's about owning your actions, matching them to your values. When accountability means keeping promises, when mistakes are seen as learning, everything changes. Missed goals can be discussed openly. No one needs to fear. This shift helps everyone focus on possibilities, not blame.

You'll notice this approach in our words. There's no jargon or buzzwords like "synergizing deliverables." Instead, you'll see terms such as "own it" (take responsibility for both wins and mistakes), "above the line" (act with curiosity and honesty, not blame), and "fail forward" (learn from setbacks instead of hiding them).

This isn't just for managers. Whether you lead, coach, volunteer, or aim for personal goals, these tools help. Accountability matters every time you promise dinner, commit to exercise, or show up for a shift. The main idea: accountability aligns words, actions, and values, improving every part of life.

Redefining Accountability for Yourself

Notice your first reaction to "accountability." Do you feel excited, curious, or supported? Does that feeling come from a mentor, friend, or yourself? Write down one area where you want more ownership and less pressure. See accountability as encouragement, not criticism. The goal isn't to judge your feelings, but to explore ways to bring about positive change.

This book shows how a new view on accountability builds trust. Instead of relying on punishments, we're moving toward a place where words, actions, and values align. No matter your background, this practical approach welcomes anyone ready to "own it" and succeed.

Drawing the Bright Line Between Accountability vs. Blame

Accountability and blame get mixed up, but they are different. Accountability is about learning and moving forward. Blame stalls progress. Imagine a missed deadline: one manager asks, "Who screwed up?" Everyone gets defensive, blames others, or goes silent. The room tenses. Another manager asks, "What happened, and how do we fix it?" Now, the focus shifts. People speak honestly and leave with a plan. That difference changes everything.

Blame feeds on accusation. In families, it sounds like, "Why can't you ever remember your chores?" instead of, "I noticed the dishes weren't done; what got in the way?" The first causes defensiveness. The second starts a conversation. Your child may admit feeling overwhelmed or forgetting, and you find solutions. In blame cultures, people fear punishment.

Employees hide mistakes or blame others. I've seen surveys where workers wrote, "If I mess up, I keep quiet because I know there will be fallout." Another said, "Everyone's just trying not to be the next scapegoat." Companies like this have high turnover and low morale.

Real accountability is proactive and helpful. It looks at actions and systems. When leading a project that misses a milestone, ask, "Let's talk about what got in the way." This language invites feedback and real solutions. Mistakes are information, not weapons.

Blame stops growth. People expect criticism and stop caring. Teams stop sharing ideas or asking for help. Forbes notes that high employee turnover signals low satisfaction and engagement. When trust is lacking and blame prevails, people feel unsupported and look for jobs elsewhere.

Accountable cultures feel different. Mistakes aren't flaws; they're events. The team finds out why and changes what's needed. People try new things, ask for help, and bounce back after setbacks.

You don't have to guess how to move from blame to accountability. You need new words and habits. Be curious, not accusing: "Let's dig into what got in the way." Offer support: "What can make this easier next time?" When someone admits a mistake, say, "Thank you for being honest. What can we learn?" Even at home, try, "Was something making it hard to get this done?" Separate actions from people.

Don't let a missed commitment define someone. Remind yourself and others: "The missed deadline isn't who you are; it's something that happened." This makes room for growth, not shame. Accountability becomes a way to learn.

Two Paths After a Missed Deadline

A regional sales team lost an important client due to a late proposal. The old manager blamed; morale dropped. People hid problems until they got worse. The new manager said, "The proposal was late. Let's review each step. Where did we get stuck? What can we change?" She listened as the team shared gaps and tight timelines. They created a checklist and set up weekly check-ins, not to micromanage, but to encourage progress. Six months later, deadlines were met, and trust flourished; the real shift: blame divided; accountability united.

Words shape reality, especially when things go wrong. When we move from blame to accountability, we build results and trust. For example, using this mindset and these examples helps us shift from finger-pointing to problem-solving in any area of life or work.

Trust First is the Hidden Engine Behind Sustainable Accountability

Accountability doesn't work without trust. Without trust, holding someone accountable feels like a threat. Teams and families then avoid accountability or do the minimum. Real, lasting accountability needs trust as its base. Otherwise, people follow rules out of fear, not from a desire to succeed together.

Imagine a volunteer group prepping for a fundraiser. In some groups, volunteers arrive late, skip meetings, and avoid tough conversations to dodge blame. Trust-based groups have honest check-ins, even when things aren't going well. People admit when they're behind and ask for help. This openness leads to better planning, teamwork, and fewer last-minute problems. The real difference lies in the trust people have in each other and in their leader.

Build trust before accountability. Start by showing vulnerability. When a leader admits a mistake, it shows that errors are normal. I've seen managers say, "I dropped the ball on our last report," and everyone relaxes. Others share struggles. This honesty makes it safe to speak up and take risks. Another simple way to build trust: keep small promises. If you say you'll send notes after a meeting, do it. If you say you'll pick up groceries, follow through. These actions build reliability that people notice. Over time, this consistency helps hold teams and families together when things get tough.

Open "level-set" conversations are another way to build trust before focusing on accountability. Start regular check-ins where everyone can say what they need and what's expected, with no surprises. In a family, this could be a Sunday night talk about everyone's schedule and what support they might need. At work, it might be a quick Monday meeting where team members share what could get in their way and where they need help. These simple habits let people bring up issues early and solve small problems before they grow.

Trust also shows in the questions you ask. Instead of saying, "Did you finish your part?" try, "Is there anything you need from me to succeed?" Even a small change, like asking, "What support would help you meet this goal?" shows you care about the person's success, not just the result.

Psychological safety is the technical term for an environment where people feel safe to take risks, admit mistakes, and ask for help without fear of humiliation or punishment. Google's Project Aristotle studied hundreds of teams. He found that psychological safety was the single biggest predictor of team effectiveness. When people felt free to speak up and share tough feedback or crazy ideas without fear, teams performed better, period. They innovated more and recovered faster from setbacks.

Stories from these teams are powerful. According to Amy C. Edmondson, psychological safety means team members feel safe to take interpersonal risks, such as admitting mistakes or challenging ideas, without fear of punishment or embarrassment. When a team lead at Google started each meeting by sharing his own mistake of the week, it encouraged others to discuss their own mistakes openly. This shift helped the team focus on solving problems together, which improved project speed and morale by fostering a culture of shared accountability and trust.

Simple habits build trust over time. Weekly "above the line" check-ins, where each person shares one thing they did to take responsibility or help someone else, keep trust strong. At home, asking your kids at dinner, "Is there anything that made your day harder?" encourages honesty instead of blame when chores are missed or tempers run high.

You don't need special programs or costly consultants to build trust. Use honest words, ask real questions, keep your promises, especially the small ones, and admit when you're wrong. These actions build trust over time and create a place where accountability feels fair and even welcome.

At your next check-in, try saying, "I'm here to help us all succeed. Is there something getting in the way that we can tackle together?" Or after a mistake, say, "I appreciate your honesty; it helps us improve as a group." When these words become normal, people stop hiding mistakes and start taking responsibility.

Trust isn't just a nice idea; it's the foundation. It makes hard conversations possible, makes expectations believable, and strengthens every commitment. Without trust, accountability is talk. With trust, accountability becomes a shared promise that everyone wants to keep.

Thinking Above the Line vs. Below the Line Helps Shifting from Excuses to Owners.

Imagine a whiteboard with a bold line across it. Above the line are phrases like "I own it," "I'll fix it," and "What can I do next?" Below the line are phrases like "It's not my fault," "Nobody told me," and "There's nothing I can do." This is called the "above the line/below the line" framework, and it clearly shows personal responsibility. Being above the line means you accept your part, step up, and look for solutions. Being below the line means avoiding, blaming, or giving up. The words and attitude you use during challenges show whether you're taking responsibility or avoiding it.

Above-the-line behavior doesn't mean you have to be perfect or always tough. It means stopping when you want to make excuses and choosing to take the next step instead. For example, a project manager who says, "We missed the mark, but here's what I'll do next time," is above the line. A manager who says, "If marketing had sent their numbers, we'd be fine," is below the line. Ownership isn't about taking all the blame; it's about seeing what you can control and acting on it.

Below-the-line thinking shows up everywhere: at work, at home, on teams, and in friendships. You hear it in skipped workouts ("It was raining and I had no ride") or missed errands ("You never reminded me"). Over time, this way of thinking weakens trust and slows progress. People start to feel powerless or expect others to fix things. Teams lose motivation, and people drift away from their goals. The ability to spark meaningful reflection and change. Start by asking yourself, after setbacks: "Was I above or below the line here?" Did I examine my role? Did I look for solutions or get stuck in excuses? In teams or families, you can use this language too: "How can we move this conversation above the line?" This simple question pivots the focus from blame to problem-solving.

In daily work, this framework acts as a quick check. After a hard meeting or a missed deadline, gather your group and ask, "Are we above or below the line on this? What's one above-the-line action each of us can take this week?" This moves the conversation from defending ourselves to taking real steps forward.

Take a tech startup that kept missing launch dates. At first, meetings were just about blaming others: engineers blamed marketing, marketing blamed product managers, and nothing got better. When the team started "above the line" reviews, each person shared one thing they'd do differently and took responsibility for a new action. Within weeks, deadlines improved, and morale rose. People stopped hiding mistakes and started solving problems together.

There is no evidence in the provided study that weekly check-ins improve volunteer attendance or reduce missed shifts at nonprofits. The cited research from Raman and colleagues focuses on how large language models can help analyze volunteer feedback in food rescue organizations. Begin meetings by having each person share one above-the-line action. Or, try daily reflection: at day's end, write down one slip below the line and how you'll act differently tomorrow. Over time, this builds awareness of avoidance and encourages decisive action.

Helpful conversations encourage ownership. When a team member makes excuses, gently ask, "What part of this can you influence?" If someone is blaming circumstances, ask, "What's one step you could still take, even if it's small?" These questions invite responsibility without blaming anyone.

The true impact isn't just productivity; it's the culture this mindset creates. Teams that think above the line trust each other more. Families who use this language handle setbacks with less resentment. People feel more confident as they build habits of action instead of making excuses. You catch yourself before slipping into blame and realign toward ownership. Teams value honesty over perfection. As this perspective spreads, meeting by meeting, reflection by reflection, you'll see more than improved results: you'll build stronger relationships and higher morale.

No matter where you are, frustrated by setbacks or eager for change, remember that moving above the line isn't about never slipping below. It's about noticing when you do and choosing differently next time. Ask yourself, "What's one area where I can move above the line today?" That's where real ownership and progress start.

Chapter Two

Mindset Reset for Building the Foundation for Change

The Mindset of "Owning It" Turns Self-Doubt into Self-Trust

You're sitting at your computer, about to make an important decision, approve something, or give honest feedback. You hesitate, recalling past mistakes or criticism. Self-doubt surfaces, and you question your abilities and your role. If this feels familiar, you're not alone.

Self-doubt often shows up as fear of mistakes, impostor syndrome, or memories of past failures. New challenges can feel like tests of your value. For new leaders, this can lead to overthinking and seeking reassurance, making it harder to feel like you belong.

When self-doubt takes over, it becomes harder to trust yourself and act. You might second-guess choices or avoid risks, which shifts focus from progress to avoiding mistakes. If you don't trust yourself, others may also struggle to trust you.

Real self-trust takes more than positive thinking. It comes from daily habits that prove self-reliance. Start with small moments of reflection. Each day, write down one thing you followed through on, like sending an email or keeping a promise. These wins build self-trust. Use any method, such as a journal or a notes app.

Another helpful approach is to set and keep micro-promises. These can be simple, like "I'll check my calendar each morning" or "I'll tidy my desk before I log off." Even if no one else notices, keeping these promises helps you build trust in yourself, no matter what others think.

To add structure, create a self-commitment contract. Write down one action to complete each day or week, sign it, and treat it like any agreement. If you miss a commitment, don't be hard on yourself. Reflect on why it happened and plan to improve next time.

Self-trust and others' trust in you are linked. When you keep promises to yourself, you become more confident with others. Your confidence grows, not because you never err, but because you can recover and restart. For example, a leader who lost credibility after missing deadlines rebuilt trust by always sending meeting notes promptly. Over time, his team found him reliable and trusted him with bigger tasks, thanks to his consistent follow-through.

Setbacks are part of life, and your self-talk matters during these times. It's easy to be self-critical, but a growth mindset is more helpful. After a mistake, shift from "I always mess up" to "I haven't mastered this yet, but I'm improving." See mistakes as learning opportunities, and trusting abilities can grow. People with this mindset persist longer and treat setbacks as progress.

When you criticize yourself, pause and consider what you'd say to a friend. We treat others with more kindness than ourselves. Try saying, "This is hard, but I can learn from it," or "Every leader starts somewhere; this is just my beginning." Kind self-talk builds resilience instead of feeding negative thoughts.

Start a Micro-Promise Tracker as a Self-Trust Builder

Each morning, set one goal for yourself, big or small, such as "I'll check in with my team by noon" or "I'll walk for ten minutes after lunch." Write it down. At day's end, record if you kept your promise and why. Weekly, review your progress, celebrate wins, and adjust if needed. Small promises kept regularly create real change.

Key Takeaway: Build self-trust by creating daily habits and making small promises to yourself. As your self-trust grows, your accountability will improve at work and in other areas of life. This new mindset helps you handle setbacks more positively, which we'll look at next. Remember: Keep promises to yourself, reflect daily, and see growth as a journey. These habits drive positive change.

Failing Forward by Using Setbacks to Accelerate Growth

Failure. Even hearing the word can be uncomfortable. We're often taught to avoid or hide it. But failure isn't a final judgment; it's feedback you can use to get better. For example, when a sales professional loses a big deal, the first impulse might be blame. Instead, they can review what happened, identify missteps, and adjust next time. Each mistake becomes a lesson and leads to improvement.

See every setback as temporary, not as identity. When you treat failure as data, it hurts less and invites curiosity. Many high achievers think this way. For example, a founder whose launch fails may first feel embarrassed, but instead reviews feedback, pinpoints errors, and consults early users to adapt. She relaunches a product that works. This is failing forward, turning setbacks into progress.

To learn from setbacks, add structure. Without reflection, you may repeat mistakes. Reflection brings clarity. After a tough week or missed goal, take a few minutes to review. Ask: What didn't go as planned? What signs did I miss? How could I improve next time? Write your thoughts, don't just think them. Teams can do this too. After missed deadlines, discuss together what happened, no blame, focus on learning.

A weekly "failure analysis" is a powerful growth tool. Use this template:

- What was my role?

- What signals did I ignore?

- What will I change this week?

Over time, you'll notice patterns, like rushing prep on Mondays or underestimating task time. Awareness of these habits helps you change.

Many successful people use failure as a stepping stone. For example, a marathon runner who doesn't finish a race doesn't quit. They review pace, hydration, and rest. Next time, they adjust training and try again. That unfinished race fuels a later best. In creative fields, writers often get rejected before publication, using each rejection as a learning opportunity.

Teams in fast fields like tech or marketing often hold "retrospectives" after projects or campaigns. These meetings focus on what went well, what didn't, and what to improve. For example, one startup shared a memo after each failed experiment, allowing others to learn from its mistakes. Taking risks is part of failing forward. It doesn't mean ignoring reality, but setting challenging, realistic goals. Smart risks push you out of your comfort zone and foster growth. Expect setbacks as part of progress, and you'll try more new things.

Regularly review your stretch goals instead of forgetting them. If you're learning a new skill at work, check in every two weeks on what's working and what needs adjustment. Record your learning in a shared document or team chat. Sharing helps normalize failure and encourages higher ambitions.

If you want to transform how you respond to setbacks, start with this exercise:

Weekly Failure Reflection

At week's end, write down one thing that didn't go as planned, big or small. Note what you wanted, what happened, and two reasons for the difference. Write one action you'll take next week based on this lesson. Small reflections lead to big changes over time.

The goal isn't to avoid failure, but to learn from it every time it happens, whether in sales, sports, creative work, or daily life. By reflecting regularly and keeping an open mind, setbacks become valuable lessons that help you grow. Embrace each setback as an opportunity to reflect, track your growth, and purposefully apply new insights. Now that you have these tools for building self-trust and growing from setbacks, let's focus on taking ownership so you can confidently rewrite your accountability story.

Rewrite Your Accountability Story by Breaking the Victim Mentality

Victim thinking is often subtle and hard to spot. It appears in your inner story when things go wrong. If you listen during tough times, you might hear, "I can't help it," "They never support me," or "It's not fair, I'm overloaded." These thoughts may feel true and bring quick relief, but they don't last. When you follow these thoughts, you give up control, slow progress, and lose ownership.

This way of thinking is common. For example, a project manager might miss a target and blame the company's culture or leadership rather than examine her own actions. Or a customer service worker might say, "Clients are impossible these days, there's nothing I can do." These reasons might sound believable, but they take away your sense of choice and control. Over time, this mindset can become a habit, leading you to focus on problems rather than solutions. Key takeaway: Notice when victim thinking appears, reclaim your choices, and prioritize solutions over blame.

The first step to breaking this cycle is to become aware of it. The next time you hear yourself say, "I'm too busy," or "My schedule won't allow it," stop and ask yourself if things are really out of your control, or if you're falling into a victim mindset. These thoughts can be so automatic that you only notice them if you pay close attention. When you spot one, call it out right away. Ask yourself, "Am I really powerless, or am I giving up my power by not looking for solutions?" This awareness helps you break old habits and start changing your story.

Reframing your thoughts is a useful way to take back control. Instead of thinking, "I can't do anything," try asking, "What's one thing I can control right now?" Even if it's just your attitude or response, having some control changes how you feel. For example, if you're stuck in traffic and running late, the victim mindset says, "This always happens to me, why bother?" The ownership mindset says, "I can call ahead and use this time to do something useful." This shift won't remove all frustration, but it helps you keep moving forward.

Narrative therapy techniques can be helpful. Take a situation where you felt powerless and rewrite the story from your own point of view, focusing on the choices you made or could have made. For example, instead of saying, "My boss gave me another last-minute task," you might say, "I accepted the task without asking for a new deadline. Next time, I'll clarify priorities before agreeing." This isn't about blaming yourself, but about taking ownership and finding new options.

Journaling and using affirmations can help you make this change. Each day, write one sentence about something you can control, even if it's small. Over time, these small actions add up and help you feel more confident in shaping your own path.

Try this exercise: Think of a recent setback that frustrated you, like a missed deadline, a tough conversation, or a disappointing outcome. First, write the story the way you usually tell it to yourself. Then, rewrite it to focus on the choices you made. Did you accept unclear instructions? Did you rush instead of asking for help? Even if your part was small, own it. This isn't about taking all the blame, but about not being a passive observer in your own life.

Real change often starts with small steps toward ownership. For example, I worked with an employee who was frustrated with her "bad bosses." She felt powerless and set up to fail. Over time, she started setting clearer boundaries and scheduling regular check-ins to manage her priorities. Even though challenges didn't disappear, she felt less resentful and more in control, shaping her experience instead of just reacting to it.

Similarly, a freelancer who was frustrated by difficult clients noticed he often thought, "Nothing I do is good enough." Once he realized this pattern, he started setting clear expectations for each project, including deadlines, deliverables, and communication. Most clients responded well, and when problems arose, he dealt with them directly rather than getting frustrated.

The words you use matter. If you catch yourself thinking, "I have no choice," try asking, "If I owned even 1% of this, what would that be?" Changing how you talk to yourself can change how you see your options and challenges.

Victim thinking doesn't disappear overnight; it sticks around because it feels comfortable. But every time you challenge these thoughts and rewrite your accountability story, you weaken their hold and make space for growth. Taking ownership of even a small part of a tough situation helps you regain your power, whether at work, at home, or anywhere else.

Making Consistency Automatic Turns Accountability into a Habit

Accountability isn't something you're born with or a badge you earn once. It's more like brushing your teeth or making coffee every day—a habit you build over time until it feels natural. If you treat accountability as a one-time effort, you'll burn out, just like trying to get fit by running once. Consistency, showing up again and again even when you're not motivated, matters more than short bursts of effort. Research shows that habits form as your brain connects repeated actions, making it easier to follow through each time. When you make accountability part of your routine, it starts to feel automatic instead of a daily struggle.

Imagine a leader who holds a short "accountability check-in" every Friday afternoon, no matter how busy things get. This isn't a big event, just a regular time to pause, review what was promised, see what was done, and set new priorities. Over time, these check-ins become a steady anchor for the team and help the leader stay disciplined. Everyone knows that each week, there's a chance to talk honestly about commitments. This simple habit creates a routine that lowers stress and builds trust.

To build habits like this for yourself or your team, start with small routines and add them to your daily or weekly schedule. Keep it simple. Begin each workday with a five-minute reflection. Write down what you planned to do, what you actually finished, and what's left for tomorrow. This quick review helps you notice patterns and catch missed commitments before they become bigger problems. Over time, these small daily pauses can lead to big improvements in consistency.

You can also add accountability to habits you already have, a method called "habit-stacking." For example, after each team meeting, have a quick "action item review" where everyone says what they'll do next. This helps people reflect and commit in front of others, making it less likely they'll forget. If you're leading a family, try a "what needs attention tomorrow?"

chat at dinner or before bed. These routines don't need to be fancy; their strength comes from doing them regularly.

Technology can help you keep these habits by making reminders easy to see and helping you avoid forgetting tasks. Apps like Todoist or Notion let you set repeating tasks, acting as digital reminders until you finish them. If you prefer paper, a checklist by your monitor or fridge works too. Some people do well with accountability partners; find someone you trust and agree to check in with a quick text each morning or night about your top priority. This is about supporting each other and making progress together, not nagging.

There are also group tools, like shared Google Sheets for tracking tasks, Slack channels for "commitment check-ins," or public whiteboards in the office where everyone writes and checks off their weekly goals. For remote teams, project management tools can send automatic reminders for updates. The important thing isn't which tool you use, but that your system keeps your promises visible and easy to remember.

The real power of habit-based accountability is how it adds up over time. Each small action, honest review, or kept promise is like adding a brick to a foundation of trust and reliability. Over weeks and months, these bricks build a strong wall that supports bigger goals and tougher challenges. It's easy to overlook the impact of small wins, but research shows they lead to major change. Building habits is like building a house brick by brick; one brick may not seem like much, but together they create something strong and lasting.

Think of this as making small improvements every day. If you get just a little better at keeping your commitments each day, those gains add up over time. You might not see big changes right away, but after a few months, you'll notice a real difference in how reliable you feel and how much others trust you.

Being consistent doesn't mean you never miss a day. It means you return to your routine after you slip up. If you miss a check-in, don't give up; just start again the next day. The goal is to keep improving, not to be perfect.

As we finish this chapter, remember that accountability gets stronger with daily practice, not just big efforts now and then. Treat it as a habit that grows and changes with your life, and you'll find it easier to stay on track, even when things get tough or distracting. In the next chapter, you'll learn how to turn these habits into systems that help you and others track progress, making accountability something everyone can share.

Chapter Three

Setting the Table for Clarity Before Commitments

Getting Everyone on the Same Page from Day One

You're on a plane about to take off. The pilot's voice comes over the intercom, but instead of a clear flight plan, all you hear is, "We'll see where we end up. Just hang in there." Instantly, your confidence crumbles. The same thing happens with teams and projects when nobody knows where they're headed or how they'll get there. That foggy uncertainty leads to missed deadlines, misunderstandings, and frustration. Whether you're leading a new team, joining a volunteer group, or starting a family project, real accountability always begins with clarity. Set expectations before any task starts. This isn't about being rigid or micromanaging. It's about making sure everyone is at the same table, with the same map and destination.

Initial alignment is the engine of every successful project. Teams fail not for lack of talent, but because no one clarified what "done" meant or who owned which part. Skipping level-setting lets assumptions run wild. One person thinks "ASAP" means next week; another thinks it means today.

Resentment brews, and deadlines slip. Proactively set the stage to prevent chaos and ensure accountability.

How do you make sure everyone starts aligned? Begin with a simple ritual at your first team meeting. I call it "table-setting." For new projects, gather everyone and state the purpose in plain language. Avoid jargon or long speeches. Say why this work matters, what's at stake, and what success looks like. Then ask each person to share what they heard and their role. This isn't a test. It's to surface hidden assumptions early. For remote or hybrid teams, do this on video. Require cameras on so faces stay visible; body language matters more when you're not sharing a room.

Use a kickoff checklist to verify all critical elements: goals, roles, timelines, communication channels, and decision authority. In one-on-one settings, discuss what success looks like, biggest worries, and past project pitfalls. Ask, "What would make this project a win?" and "Where have things gone wrong before?" Surface hidden expectations proactively.

Documentation is your ally. Don't trust memory for critical agreements. At the start of each project, open a shared Google Doc or Notion page and note what's been decided: ownership, deadlines, and update processes. For bigger projects, create a simple visual charter with goals, deliverables, owners, and milestones. The goal isn't bureaucracy. It's to have one source of truth when confusion arises.

As projects move forward, don't treat these agreements as relics. Level-setting isn't a one-and-done event; it needs periodic maintenance. Build in mid-project "temperature checks." These are short meetings where everyone reviews what's working and what needs tweaking. Schedule these after major milestones or whenever things start to feel off track. Ask directly: "Do we all still agree on what success looks like?" "Has anything changed that means we need to adjust roles or timelines?" When priorities shift, or new information comes in (and it always does), hold a realignment session. Update your shared doc or project charter together. This keeps everyone rowing in the same direction and prevents drift.

Team Kickoff Checklist

When you launch a new project or a family goal, follow this checklist step by step. Clearly identify each person's primary role and specific responsibility for the project or goal.

- Discuss and agree on project deadlines, and decide together who will have the authority to make final decisions.

- Talk as a group about which communication tools to use. Decide together if Slack, text messaging, or in-person check-ins will be your main way to communicate.

- Choose a simple method everyone will use to track progress, such as a shared document or a task board, and make sure everyone understands how to use it.

- Agree together on how and when feedback will be shared among the group. Decide whether it will happen during meetings, in writing, or in one-on-one conversations.

After reviewing the checklist, have each person state their role and deadlines in their own words. Record these answers and share them with the team to guarantee everyone understands and agrees.

Refer to initial agreements throughout the project. Keep expectations visible, revisit them often, and clearly communicate any changes. This transparency fosters trust and ownership, making teams more effective under pressure.

What Really Matters is Defining Outcomes, Not Just Outputs

You can spend hours in meetings, crank out dozens of reports, and still feel like nothing's moving forward. That's the trap of focusing on outputs instead of outcomes. Outputs are the tasks, sending a weekly status email, ticking off action items, and cleaning the kitchen. Outcomes are the results that actually matter: a team that's informed and aligned, a project that lands on time, a home that feels calm and welcoming. Too many teams, families, and even friendships get stuck in that grind. Everyone's busy, but progress is an illusion. The difference between checking boxes and achieving something real is not just technical; it's foundational to accountability.

When you only measure activity, you set yourself up for disappointment. Imagine a marketing team that produces stacks of social posts and multiple newsletters, and hosts three webinars, all on time and according to plan. The project board looks impressive. But the real goal was to bring in new leads, and that number barely moved. All those outputs, hours spent, tasks completed, don't add up to the outcome that matters. Or picture the classic family chore chart. Every task has a checkmark, but the house still feels chaotic because nobody agreed on what "clean" means or why it matters. People become frustrated, wondering why all that effort isn't translating into better results.

Flip the script by defining success in terms of impact. Before assigning tasks or deadlines, ask: What's the real win here? What will be different if we get this right? This re-focuses work on impact instead of activity.

I use a simple framework for outcome-driven goals: make them SMART, but always tie them back to impact. That means being Specific, Measurable, Achievable, Relevant, and Time-bound. But don't stop at numbers alone. Ask what will actually change if you hit those numbers. For example: instead of "Hold three client events this quarter," try "Increase customer retention by 10% by holding three targeted client events and following up with personalized check-ins." The second version ties action to purpose. It's not just about activity, but about the result those activities are meant to drive.

Start each planning meeting by asking, "What does a win look like for us?" Push for concrete answers. If unsure, follow up with, "How will we know when we're successful?" These actions force clarity and alignment. People aim for real change that they can measure.

When spelling out outcomes with others, clarity is always more important than complexity. Avoid buzzwords or sweeping statements like "drive engagement" or "improve performance." Instead, describe the end state: "Our customers will call us first when they need help," or "Our meetings will end with every person knowing their next step." If you're working with kids or volunteers, keep it even simpler. Say: "The living room will be tidy enough for us to have guests over without rushing to clean up," or "Everyone will know their schedule by Monday morning."

Scripts help keep these conversations focused and positive. I often use questions like, "If we do all this work but nothing changes for our customers (or our family), what would we wish we'd done differently?" Or "Let's imagine it's Friday. How will we know this week was a success?" These prompts move talk away from just listing tasks and toward painting a clear picture of progress.

Misaligned or unclear outcomes breed frustration and wasted effort. I've watched organizations spend months rolling out new software. Everyone followed the plan exactly, but because no one defined what a successful launch actually meant for users, adoption lagged, and complaints piled up. In another case, a nonprofit spent weeks planning events to "raise awareness," but never decided what awareness would look like in action. After all the effort, attendance stayed flat, and donations didn't budge. The lesson is simple: when nobody knows the true purpose or result, you end up with lots of motion but no movement.

Avoid this trap by making outcomes visible and revisiting them often. Write them down at the top of every project doc or meeting agenda. Check in weekly: "Are we moving closer to our real goal?" If things veer off course, don't just push harder on tasks. Instead, pause and ask if everyone still agrees on what matters most.

This shift from outputs to outcomes changes everything about how people show up and hold themselves accountable. It gives meaning to daily tasks and helps teams and families rally together when things get tough. Instead of measuring worth by how much you did, you start measuring by whether you made a difference. That's where real accountability takes root.

Scripts for Setting Expectations Without Jargon and Using Language That Sticks

How you communicate expectations makes all the difference in accountability. Relying on jargon, buzzwords, or vague business-speak only leads to confusion. I've watched teams nod along to phrases like, "Let's circle back and leverage some synergistic KPIs," only to walk away unclear about what's actually required and when. Jargon doesn't create clarity; it often leaves people hesitant to ask questions or embarrassed to admit confusion. If you want people to buy in and follow through, use straightforward language. Don't hide behind labels. Direct, clear speech makes it easier for everyone, regardless of background, to understand what's needed.

Notice the difference between "Let's optimize our workflow deliverables by EOD" and "Please send me your edits by 5 PM today." The first is vague, while the second leaves no room for confusion. Clarity isn't just politeness; it builds a culture where commitments are visible, and everyone knows their role. Compare telling a child, "Tidy your zone proactively each evening," versus "Please put your toys away before dinner." Abstract language leads to tuning out or misinterpretation, which is how things fall through the cracks.

When setting expectations as a manager, use: "By Friday at 3 PM, please send the report to the team." Peer-to-peer: "Can you handle client emails while I'm out on Thursday?" At home: "I'll need your help with cleanup right after dinner." For volunteers: "Let's meet at the front desk by 8:45 AM for setup." These sentences don't just clarify the action; they demonstrate respect for people's time, remove wiggle room that leads to missed commitments, and prevent resentment.

Checking for understanding is just as critical as giving clear instructions. Many leaders and parents assume spoken words equal commitment; in reality, agreement often isn't comprehension. You might say, "Finish the presentation slides and update the budget," but unless you verify that the message landed, you may be surprised by what gets delivered. Change the game by following an expectation with, "Can you repeat back what you'll be doing and by when?" This isn't patronizing. If done right, it's collaborative and helps surface any confusion early. Other helpful questions: "What challenges do you see with this plan?" or "Does any part feel unclear or risky?" These invite honest feedback and address problems before they escalate.

Parents use this with teens who often "forget" chores: "So tell me what your plan is for laundry this week." When teens respond in their own words, you know you've been heard, and if not, clarification happens without accusations. In work settings, this prevents awkwardness when someone quietly doesn't understand but is afraid to speak up. For volunteers or committees, ending meetings with a check-in ("Let's each share our next step and deadline") ensures everyone leaves aligned.

Reinforcing verbal expectations visually boosts follow-through. Relying on memory is risky because people have plenty on their minds, distractions are ever-present, and good intentions can fade quickly. That's why summary emails after meetings are effective; they lay out agreements so no one is left guessing. Simple bullet points outlining who's responsible for what, and by when, keep everyone honest. Screenshots of project boards like Trello or Asana, shared in team chats or pinned to digital boards, keep tasks visible and top of mind.

In homes, sticky notes on the fridge or shared family calendars help everyone remember their promises. Some families snap photos of completed chores, a clean kitchen, and an organized garage, and share them in a group chat as both proof and encouragement. Visual cues offer gentle reminders, reducing the need for nagging and replacing it with shared pride in getting things done.

For volunteer groups or clubs, a public checklist shown at meetings or shared online keeps everyone in the loop. When people see their names next to tasks and deadlines, it motivates follow-through and makes accountability visible without confrontation.

To build this habit, start small. After any conversation where expectations are set at work, at home, or with a community group, pause to check back: "What's your next step?" Then document it clearly for both parties. Over time, this becomes routine. People start to expect and request it because it removes uncertainty and builds trust.

Language shapes how people feel about their roles and responsibilities. Remove jargon, use direct language, and ensure every expectation is spoken, seen, and checked for understanding. When communication is this clear, accountability becomes a natural, shared habit instead of a struggle.

Holding Space for Creating Safety in Candid Conversations

Holding space means fostering an environment where people feel safe to speak honestly, admit mistakes, and address tough issues without embarrassment or fear of backlash. It requires more than just good listening; true holding space is shown through your words, reactions, and body language. This demonstrates that you genuinely welcome truth, even when it's uncomfortable. Psychological safety is essential for real accountability. Without it, people hide errors, sugarcoat problems, and withhold information. Tension leads to defensiveness, and accountability suffers. The leader's task, whether you're a boss, parent, or organizer, is to make it clear that honesty is not punished, and everyone benefits from truth being brought to the table.

For instance, I once worked with a team where a member finally admitted a significant oversight after months of stress and missed targets. What changed? The leader started every Monday meeting with a simple ritual:

everyone shared something that made them anxious about the upcoming week. Initially, this was awkward, as nobody wanted to appear weak. But as the practice continued, people began opening up about real worries. The turning point came when a quiet team member confessed, "I need to admit I dropped the ball on last month's report. I was afraid to say anything." Instead of blaming, the leader paused, thanked the person for their honesty, and asked how the team could help fix the issue together. This established a new tone where honesty was expected and necessary, not risky.

To build this kind of safety, rituals and ground rules help. Start meetings with a question like, "What's one thing you're worried about right now?" or "Is there something you wish you could say but haven't?" These openers normalize vulnerability, showing that nobody is expected to be perfect. In family or community settings, use a weekly check-in where each person shares a challenge without interruptions. Ground rules such as "no interrupting" and "no shaming" should be agreed upon and visible. These aren't just procedural; they create a culture where candor is valued, and feedback doesn't devolve into blame.

Responding non-defensively to tough news is crucial as a leader. If someone admits a mistake or gives difficult feedback, your first reaction will shape future conversations. Keep supportive phrases ready, like, "Thank you for telling me. What do you need from me right now?" or, "Let's work through this together." Your body language matters, too: maintain an open posture, nod as they speak, and keep steady eye contact without glaring. These cues lower defenses and show you're listening with empathy, not waiting to criticize.

Sometimes, you'll hear things that sting. This might be direct criticism or an admission that someone didn't trust you enough to come forward sooner. Resist the urge to get defensive. Instead, pause and say, "I appreciate your honesty," or, "That's hard to hear, but I'm glad you said it." If you feel yourself becoming reactive, take a breath and remember that discomfort is part of everyone's growth process.

Of course, nobody handles these moments perfectly every time. You might snap or make a sarcastic comment that shuts down the conversation. Repairing trust after safety is breached is as important as establishing it in the first place. Immediately own your mistake: "That came out wrong. I apologize." Avoid minimizing the issue; a sincere apology resets the tone and re-invites openness. Follow up if needed: "I want you to know I value your input, even when I react poorly." People are willing to forgive if they see you taking responsibility quickly.

If someone goes quiet after a tense moment, check in privately: "I noticed I got short with you earlier. I'm sorry. Is there anything I can do to make it right?" This humility signals that maintaining trust is more important than protecting your ego. Over time, these small repairs strengthen relationships and make it easier for others to speak up in the future.

Holding space isn't soft. It's demanding, requiring patience, self-awareness, and ongoing effort. But when people know they won't be punished for telling the truth, they're more likely to surface problems early, before they escalate. You'll see more genuine conversations about what's working and what isn't, whether at work, at home, or anywhere people come together to achieve something.

To conclude: clarity sets expectations, but safety sustains them. Accountability flourishes when people are seen and heard, and when mistakes are met with curiosity rather than criticism. As you move on to building systems to track habits and progress, remember this foundation: honesty thrives where leaders consistently hold space for every voice.

Chapter Four

The Plug-and-Play Accountability System

The Four Pillars are Expectation, Check-In, Consequence, Repair

Picture having dinner with friends, family, or volunteers, talking about big goals like earning a certification, starting a new project, or spending more time together. The ambition is there, but after a few weeks, those promises often fade. This usually happens not because people don't care, but because there isn't a system tailored to each context to turn talk into action. The Four Pillars of accountability, Expectation, Check-In, Consequence, and Repair, offer a repeatable process that helps make intentions real across different settings.

The first pillar is **Expectation**, a crucial starting point for accountability. Before moving to the next pillar, it's important to ensure expectations are not just handed out, but are clear about what needs to be done, who will do it, when it's due, and why it matters. Explaining the reason behind a task gives it purpose. If you're in charge, set deadlines and explain what's at stake. This kind of clarity helps prevent confusion and half-hearted effort. Make sure everyone knows their roles and what's expected, and write down agreements in an email, shared document, or voice memo so you don't have to rely on memory.

Once expectations are set, move to the next pillar: **Check-In**. Regular reviews are important because waiting until problems appear can slow things down. Set up checkpoints like weekly meetings, biweekly catch-ups, or quick progress emails. The goal isn't to micromanage, but to give people a chance to talk about obstacles and share progress. Check-ins should make it easy for people to say when they're stuck and ask for help without feeling blamed. If you skip check-ins, it can send the message that accountability doesn't matter.

After establishing a rhythm of regular check-ins, focus on the third pillar: **Consequence**. This step is often misunderstood or avoided. It's not about punishment, but about reinforcing commitments in a way that builds confidence. Recognize people who follow through, and if possible, do it publicly with praise or rewards. When someone misses a commitment, respond by setting a new timeline, redistributing tasks, or having a conversation about what happened. The goal isn't to shame anyone, but to make sure actions matter and everyone's promises are valued, which can motivate your team to stay engaged.

If things don't go as planned, shift to the fourth pillar: **Repair**. This is where genuine trust is built. No system is perfect. Deadlines get missed, mistakes happen, and sometimes feelings are hurt. Repair means addressing problems honestly rather than letting resentment build. Admitting mistakes, asking for feedback, or suggesting solutions shows respect and courage. Repair is not just about fixing problems; it also strengthens teams and relationships over time, fostering a sense of safety and support among your audience.

These pillars work together. Set expectations by clarifying who does what, by when, and why. Check in regularly, follow through with consequences, celebrate successes, and adjust as needed. To ensure your system is effective, track progress using simple metrics such as completed tasks, missed deadlines, and team member feedback. When things go wrong, repair:

recognize the problem, discuss how to improve without blaming, and agree on a better approach. Repeat the cycle. Each round builds more trust and reliability, and measuring results helps refine your process over time.

The Accountability Cycle Flowchart

Expectation → Check-In → Consequence → Repair

This closed cycle keeps relationships strong, with each part supporting the next.

- Be clear about actions needed.

- Assign clear responsibility.

- Set a due date.

- Explain the reason.

- Have each person confirm their role.

- Record the agreement.

Then follow up by:

- Keep check-ins brief: What was done?

- Name obstacles: "What's in the way?"

- Review deadlines and commitments.

- Confirm next steps and changes.

Talk about consequences ahead of time, including both positive ones like "Let's celebrate this milestone!" and corrective ones such as "If we miss it again, let's revisit our approach." Make sure everyone understands what will happen if things get off track.

Starting repair after something goes wrong can feel awkward, but it's important for building real trust. You might begin by saying, "We missed our goal. Let's talk openly about what happened and how to get back on track." Ask for feedback on what changes could help.

The real value of these pillars goes beyond just reaching goals; they help create psychological safety, which is essential for strong teams and families. When people know that mistakes won't be punished but will be discussed openly, they are more likely to speak up and solve problems quickly. Teams that repair a regular habit recover faster from mistakes, rather than letting issues turn into grudges or gossip.

These pillars work at home as well. Families who check in weekly about chores or plans can avoid resentment. When things go wrong, honest repair conversations help restore connection instead of letting frustration grow. In any setting, this system isn't extra work. It's what makes reliability and trust possible without losing the human touch.

Accountability Blueprints for Teams, Volunteers, and Families

Accountability looks different at work, at home, and in volunteer groups, but each can benefit from a system that fits its style. The key is to build on structure without forcing everyone into the same mold. On workplace teams, accountability works best with clear visibility and regular routines. Imagine a group starting the week with a 'sprint kickoff' where each person shares their main commitment out loud, no hiding or confusion. For example, you might say, 'Let's each share one big action item for this week and check back on Friday.' These public commitments, along with a tracking board or dashboard everyone can see, create social pressure and clarity. At week's end, the team reviews what was accomplished, what got stuck, and what needs support. If someone falls behind, the group does not blame; they ask what happened and how to help. This openness keeps the momentum going and prevents misunderstandings.

In volunteer groups such as church committees, event crews, or neighborhood clean-ups, the system should remain flexible to match changing availability and motivation. Accountability in these settings relies on mutual respect and clear agreements rather than formal authority. Simple tools work best: sign-up sheets for tasks, rotating roles, and group text reminders to ensure nothing is forgotten. A coordinator might message, "Who can bring snacks for Saturday? Let's confirm by Wednesday." This prompt offers individuals the chance to step up. Assigning roles in advance, even for small actions, ensures involvement. If commitments are overlooked, use gentle reminders like, "Just checking if you're still able to cover setup this weekend." When reminders come from both peers and leaders, participation tends to remain steady.

Family life is different. You can't fire anyone or leave when things get tense. Instead of dashboards and emails, families use visual reminders and conversations. A chore chart lists daily or weekly tasks. Rewards motivate kids, like, 'If you finish your chores by Saturday, you pick the movie.' For teens or adults, consequences might mean swapping tasks or taking turns with dinner duty. Family meetings should be short, predictable, and held when there's no conflict. These are for setting and checking expectations. Everyone gets to speak, frustrations are shared early, and successes are celebrated. The goal isn't control, but keeping communication open so problems don't build up.

The formality of your system should depend on your group's size and culture. For fast-paced teams or organizations with high stakes, use formal tools such as shared spreadsheets, written agreements, or weekly reports to track work and avoid forgetting. Volunteers who dislike structure use informal methods like WhatsApp reminders, quick verbal check-ins, and sticky notes for tasks. Families benefit from visual trackers, like whiteboards for chores or color-coded calendars for activities, so everyone can see what needs to be done and no one can say they didn't know.

Troubleshooting is necessary everywhere. Teams often lose momentum after missing check-ins; energy fades, and things slow down. To restart, make meetings shorter and focus on one commitment per person. This reduces overwhelm and helps people follow through. If someone keeps missing tasks, talk privately and ask what support they need, rather than calling them out.

Volunteer groups often navigate burnout and fluctuating participation. When involvement drops or motivation wanes, rotate responsibilities more frequently to prevent anyone from feeling stuck. Publicly acknowledge efforts through thank-you notes or group chat shout-outs, and always prepare backup plans for important roles to ensure events run smoothly. If reminders are ineffective, adjust the approach, try switching from emails to texts or phone calls to see what works for your group.

Families encounter their own accountability challenges, such as members frequently forgetting duties or citing busy schedules. If certain chores are repeatedly overlooked, hold a brief family meeting to discuss possible task swaps or brainstorm more manageable routines. Visual cues, like placing shoes near the door to prompt taking out the trash, or turning chores into a game with points for consecutive completions, can help foster engagement and follow-through.

Having scripts can help when you're not sure what to say. In teams, you might ask, 'What do you need to hit your goal this week?' In volunteer groups, try, 'Is anyone able to swap roles if something comes up at the last minute?' In families, ask, 'What's getting in the way of finishing your part? Let's figure it out together.' These kinds of questions help people feel safe and encourage problem-solving instead of making excuses.

No matter where you are, at work, with a volunteer group, or at home, the best accountability systems are the ones that fit your group's style and respect everyone's needs. Formal systems are only helpful if they clarify and make it easier to act; otherwise, simple check-ins work just as well. The goal isn't to be perfect, but to keep making progress and communicate honestly, especially when things get messy.

Customizing the System for Startups, Nonprofits, and Remote Work

Startups thrive on change. Priorities shift quickly, new opportunities come up, and one meeting can change the direction of a project. In this fast-paced environment, accountability often gets pushed aside because teams feel too busy for structure. But having clarity is essential, even in the chaos. The system adapts by focusing on visibility and flexibility: leaders can set up shared Slack channels for posting daily or weekly goals, and tools like Notion or Asana can keep all tasks in one place. When things change, everyone updates the shared workspace to keep the team on the same page. Short, focused meetings, no longer than fifteen minutes, help people share what's blocking them or changes in roles. These routines don't slow things down; they help everyone stay coordinated as the company deals with constant change. Even with tight deadlines, a dynamic task board where everyone is responsible for their part helps spot problems and avoid taking on too much. One startup I worked with cut wasted effort in half just by adding a Monday 'reset' meeting to confirm weekly priorities and update the board as new projects came up.

Nonprofits face unique challenges, such as limited resources, fluctuating volunteer availability, and the ongoing need to maintain morale, especially when tasks aren't exciting. In these settings, accountability works best when it's grounded in mutual respect and a shared purpose, not in strict rules. Google Sheets is a practical, low-cost tool for tracking sign-ups and progress. Trello boards can help manage events by assigning color-coded cards for each volunteer's role as people confirm or swap shifts. Doodle polls make it easy to find meeting times that work for everyone. Group check-ins work best as supportive gatherings instead of formal reviews. I worked with a nonprofit that increased event turnout by pairing new volunteers with 'buddies' and encouraging midweek and pre-event check-ins, thereby reducing no-shows and building a sense of community.

Remote work brings its own set of challenges, like different time zones, digital fatigue, cultural differences, and the temptation to check out when no one is watching. Accountability in this setting relies on transparency and tools that don't require everyone to be online at the same time. Shared calendars help everyone stay up to date on deadlines and important meetings, no matter where they are. Check-ins can happen on Zoom or Google Meet, but they don't always have to be live; a Loom video update works for any time zone. Shared documents, such as living agendas and running question lists, keep the team connected between meetings. Clear 'working agreements' set expectations for response times, core hours, and how to show when someone is offline. Scheduling check-ins that respect local holidays or traditions shows cultural awareness and helps prevent burnout.

When choosing tech tools, focus on what's practical. Startups often like Slack because it's fast and integrates with other tools. It can automate reminders, host standups in threads, and highlight urgent issues. Notion's wiki setup makes it easy to update as goals change. Asana is great for showing sprints and dependencies, providing a clear timeline for everyone. For nonprofits, Google Sheets is a flexible, free tool for tracking volunteers, budgets, and contacts. Trello is popular for its drag-and-drop boards, which are good for volunteers who don't like spreadsheets. Doodle makes scheduling meetings easier by letting everyone vote on the best times.

Remote teams need tools that help people connect without overwhelming them. Zoom check-ins are useful, but shouldn't take up too much time on the calendar. Online calendars like Outlook or Google Calendar help everyone see when they can work together. Loom videos are helpful for leaders who want to add a personal touch by sharing screen-recorded recaps or 'state of the team' messages, so everyone stays informed even if they miss live meetings.

Global teams have to put extra effort into communication because cultural differences can affect how people exterpret deadlines, feedback, or even silence in messages. In these cases, working agreements help clarify expectations for how quickly people should respond, encourage the use of clear language rather than jargon, and ensure important decisions are documented openly. Using a shared calendar to recognize different holidays helps make sure no one feels pressured to work during their own observances.

Mini case studies show how tailoring these principles can make a difference. One startup that struggled with shifting projects reduced missed deadlines by 40% after switching from random Slack chats to weekly Asana check-ins, which made project scope changes clear and open for discussion. A nonprofit with low volunteer morale saw participation rise after introducing a 'buddy' system, which helped people feel valued and supported. In a remote-first tech company, moving from written updates to short Loom video recaps increased team engagement, as people felt more connected even if they never met in person.

In any setting, whether it's a startup, nonprofit, or remote team, the key is to choose tools that fit your workflow, make communication clear, and set up routines that match your culture. Accountability isn't about micromanaging, but about creating reliable habits that make it easy to follow through, even when things are always changing.

Overcoming "We're Too Small for Systems" and Other Size Myths

People often think accountability systems are just for big companies with HR departments, lots of managers, and too many meetings. If you're running a two-person business, freelancing, or managing a busy family, it's easy to believe that structure would slow you down or take away your flexibility. But the truth is, size doesn't matter when it comes to needing clarity. Even solo entrepreneurs benefit from having some process. I know a freelance designer who uses a simple wall-mounted Kanban board to track projects. Every client deliverable gets its own sticky note, moving from 'in progress' to 'sent' to 'paid.' That small bit of structure means fewer missed deadlines, less searching for lost feedback, and a better reputation with clients. The same idea works for two business partners juggling side projects. They might use a shared to-do list app to keep track of who's handling proposals or billing each week. When both people can see the list, there's less finger-pointing and more progress.

The real secret is to make the system the right size for your needs, so it helps you without taking up too much time or blocking your creativity. You don't need lots of forms or endless spreadsheets. Short check-ins, like a ten-minute meeting at the start or end of the day, can really help small teams stay clear on priorities. These don't need a set agenda, just a quick review of what's important, any open questions, and a chance to spot anything that could cause problems tomorrow. For people who like visuals, a few sticky notes on the fridge or a whiteboard can be more effective than any app. Each person writes their main tasks or goals for the week and moves them as they make progress. This hands-on approach keeps priorities clear without cluttering your phone or inbox.

People often resist systems, saying they don't have time or that it feels like too much. I hear this all the time from small nonprofits, family businesses, and even roommates sharing chores. But the truth is, not having structure usually ends up costing more time. Missed bills, forgotten calls, and double-booked appointments happen not because people are lazy, but because no one wants to nag or be nagged. The solution doesn't have to be complicated. A one-page accountability agreement can quickly clarify expectations: what needs to be done, who is responsible, and by when. This paper or digital agreement isn't about policing; it's a memory aid and a shared promise. On busy days, a five-minute end-of-day review to check what got done and what needs attention tomorrow can prevent confusion before it turns into bigger problems.

One of the biggest mindset shifts is realizing that systems strengthen relationships rather than replace them. Many people worry that adding structure will take away spontaneity or make everything feel like a chore. In reality, structure protects your time and attention, letting you focus on fun, creative work or relax, with fewer distractions. I know a family who used to argue about chores every Saturday morning. After they started using a simple whiteboard where everyone chose their own tasks for the week, the arguments stopped, and weekends felt easier. They even found they had more time for movie nights because no one was upset about 'who always does more.' I've also seen a small nonprofit keep more volunteers just by checking in regularly, not with long meetings, but with quick calls or texts to say 'thanks' or ask how things are going. People felt noticed and valued, not forgotten.

Structure doesn't have to mean bureaucracy. The best systems are usually invisible, only showing up when you need them. For example, two friends running an online shop set aside Friday afternoons for a 'state of the business' chat. It's just 15 minutes to catch up on orders, divide tasks for the next week, and flag any customer issues. This routine saves them hours of back-and-forth texting during the week and helps prevent things from slipping through the cracks when they get busy.

If you're still unsure, try starting with the bare minimum: a shared checklist for the week's main tasks (at work or at home), a regular five-minute check-in before everyone leaves in the morning, or a quick end-of-day review where each person shares one thing they finished and one thing they still need to do. See how it feels after two weeks. Most people notice less stress and more clarity right away.

The point isn't to copy what big organizations do, but to use what's helpful in ways that fit your life or team. You can always add more structure if things get complicated, or simplify if everything is running smoothly.

As we finish this chapter, remember that accountability isn't about size or formality. It's about being reliable and showing respect for yourself and others. Even solo businesses and families deserve the peace of knowing what's done, what's next, and who's responsible. Simple, intentional processes keep things running smoothly and let you spend less time worrying about missed tasks and more time enjoying the work and people that matter most. Next, we'll look at how to keep your momentum strong when stress or distractions threaten your plans.

Chapter Five

Turning Talk into Action by Tracking, Follow-Through, and Feedback

Assigning, Documenting, and Delegating an Action Item Architecture

Meetings end with ideas but rarely with clear action, so nothing happens. For results, specify and make action items visible. Avoid vague promises. Only clear commitments drive progress.

A strong action item must clearly state who is responsible, what is to be done, when it will be completed, and why it matters. For example: "Chris will upload last month's expenses by Friday noon for Monday's review." Clarity in assignments builds accountability.

Templates can help. Try using "action item cards," digital or on paper. Each card should include the owner's name, a one-sentence task, a deadline, and a way to measure success. Ask, "How will we know it's done?" For complex projects, use a RACI chart. It shows who is Responsible (does the work), Accountable (owns the outcome), Consulted (gives input), and Informed (gets updates). This simple system cuts confusion. It stops people from saying, "I didn't realize that was my job."

Documentation makes commitments real. When you document action items in a plan, writing them down makes them real. Place them somewhere everyone can see, such as a shared Google Sheet, a Trello board, or even a whiteboard at home or work. This turns promises into visible progress. Being open about tasks creates gentle pressure and builds trust. After each meeting, send a summary email that lists who is responsible for what and by when. Make these commitments stand out so they don't get lost in long emails. If you use digital tools, tag people directly so no one misses their tasks. Keeping an up-to-date action log helps everyone stay honest and makes it harder to let things slip. True delegation is about empowering others to own outcomes, not just check off to-dos. Describe the desired result instead of micromanaging every step. Say, "I'd like you to handle organizing next month's team lunch. Your goal is to have everyone's dietary needs covered and send out invites by next Friday." Then ask, "What support do you need from me?" or "How do you plan to tackle this?" These questions show trust and invite initiative.

Making sure everyone understands is just as important as giving directions. Always check that your expectations are clear. Ask the person to repeat back what they'll do and when they'll update you. This isn't about talking down to anyone; it's about making sure things are clear. If someone seems unsure or confused, take time to explain before problems start.

A Clarity Checklist

After your next meeting or planning session, use this quick checklist to review the clarity of your action items before moving forward. For each item, ask yourself:

* Does it clearly state the task?

- Does it state who is responsible?

- Is it logged somewhere visible to the whole team?

- Does everyone understand why it matters?

If you answer "no" to any question, revise before moving forward.

When you consistently create specific action items, document them, and delegate with trust, confusion is replaced by clarity, and empty promises become real, measurable progress. With this foundation in place, it's essential to maintain momentum. This leads naturally into the next section: using meaningful check-ins to keep everyone aligned and accountable.

The Art of the Check-In Using Scripts for Meaningful Progress Updates

Meaningful check-ins surface obstacles, celebrate progress, and create space for honest conversation. Routine status updates often miss what matters: where things are stuck and the support needed. Real accountability grows from transparency and problem-solving, not from repetitive box-ticking.

A meaningful check-in starts by asking the right questions. Instead of just giving a summary of work, ask things like: "What's working? What's stuck? What do you need?" These prompts help people talk about both successes and challenges. This leads to real conversations, not just ticking boxes. This approach works in team meetings, one-on-ones, or even a quick message with an accountability partner. It's flexible. For a Monday team huddle, try: "Let's go around and share one thing that moved forward last week, anything you're stuck on now, and one area where you could use help." This opens up conversation while keeping it non-threatening. For remote or distributed teams, asynchronous check-ins work just as well. Use a simple template in Slack or another chat tool: "Share your top win from last week, one thing holding you back, and any support you need this week." People can chime in when convenient. Everyone stays up to date, no matter where they are.

Peer accountability thrives on honest questions. In a check-in with an accountability partner, skip small talk and ask, "What's your biggest win since we last talked? Where did you struggle? What's your next step?" These keep focus on real progress.

Timing matters. Too many check-ins can feel like micromanagement. Too few allow problems to fester. Weekly check-ins keep momentum without becoming a burden. For some projects, biweekly or milestone-based check-ins work best, especially if tied to deliverables. Quick daily "standups" help fast teams stay on track. Monthly check-ins support reflection and strategy.

Check-ins are most useful when they uncover blockers early. Make it safe to bring up issues by asking directly: "What's getting in your way?" or "Is there a decision or resource that would help you move forward?" If someone is hesitant or vague, prompt gently: "Can you say a bit more about what's making this tough?" or "Would you like help brainstorming?"

The most effective check-ins mix structure with openness. Hold them regularly so everyone knows what to expect, but stay flexible to dig deeper when needed. If someone shares a struggle, others are more likely to open up if they feel safe and supported. When progress slows, use the check-in to find solutions together rather than blame anyone. Ask, "What can we try differently this week?" or "Who else could help out?" This builds a team mindset focused on solving problems, not pointing fingers. To make check-ins something your team or family looks forward to, ensure each one feels purposeful and energized. Give recognition for effort, not just results. Remember: meaningful check-ins aren't just about tracking tasks. They're about people connecting and working together toward shared goals.

Once you're tracking progress with regular check-ins, choose the right tool to visualize and manage progress. With so many apps and old-school methods, picking one can be tough. Digital tools like Trello, Asana,

Notion, and Google Sheets offer instant updates and shared access. You can move cards on a Kanban board, color-code tasks, and tag teammates for teamwork in real time. These platforms work well for remote teams or complex projects where everyone needs visibility into progress. Features like deadlines, reminders, emojis, and links to calendars or chat apps keep things moving and make status checks easy. But digital tools need regular updates to work. If you don't keep them current, they lose value quickly. Notifications can also get lost in busy inboxes or be ignored as spam.

Analog tracking, like whiteboards, sticky notes, and paper planners, offers a different kind of satisfaction. Moving a sticky note from "To Do" to "Done" or checking off a box in your planner feels rewarding in a way digital tools sometimes can't match. For individuals or small groups in the same space, a whiteboard in the kitchen or office keeps everyone accountable. Written progress builds a stronger mental link than digital taps, and there's no risk of forgotten passwords. However, analog systems are harder to share over long distances, require manual updates, and can become messy or be ignored when busy. Choose based on your needs—digital dashboards suit those who prefer notifications and visuals, while analog methods appeal to those who want something tangible and always visible. Many people even blend both: a Trello board at work and a paper calendar at home.

Analog tracking, like whiteboards, sticky notes, and paper planners, offers a different kind of satisfaction. Moving a sticky note from "To Do" to "Done" or checking off a box in your planner feels rewarding. Digital tools sometimes can't match this. For individuals or small groups in the same space, a whiteboard in the kitchen or office keeps everyone accountable. It's hard to ignore a task that stays in the "Not Started" column day after day. Paper trackers are great for building habits. Writing down your progress creates a stronger mental link than tapping a screen. There's also no risk of tech problems or forgotten passwords. However, analog systems are harder to share over distance. They need manual updates and can get messy or overlooked during busy times. When picking between these worlds, consider both your context and your personality. Are you energized by digital notifications and love data-driven visuals? Digital dashboards might be your friend. Do you crave the tactile satisfaction of pen on paper or want something visible without another login? Go analog. Some people even blend both approaches. For example, use a Trello board at work to track personal habits while using a paper calendar at home.

Setting up visual dashboards can be simple. For teams, a Kanban board with "To Do," "Doing," and "Done" columns keeps priorities clear. Each card has a task and an owner, and moving it across the board builds accountability and a sense of progress. For personal goals, use a habit-tracking calendar where you color in or check off each day you stick to your plan. Research shows that marking progress this way helps you follow through and remember better. These simple visuals make your effort visible and worth celebrating.

Real-world setups prove how adaptable tracking can be. I've worked with nonprofits that transformed volunteer engagement by creating massive wall charts, each shift gets a box, and every volunteer signs off as they complete their commitment. The chart is public, colorful, and becomes a point of pride as it fills up, making participation contagious. In contrast, a remote software team I coached uses shared digital dashboards in Notion, complete with emoji status updates for each project. Team members update their progress asynchronously; anyone can scan the board to see who's on track or needs help, cutting down on endless status meetings.

Even the best tracker won't work if you don't keep it up to date. Tracker fatigue happens when updates feel like a chore or don't seem useful. To avoid this, make tracker reviews part of your regular meetings and treat them as a routine, not an afterthought. Change who manages the tracker each week so no one gets stuck with extra work and everyone feels involved. If your system starts to feel cluttered or overwhelming, simplify it: remove extra columns, clear out old tasks, or try a new format. The best trackers are the ones you actually want to use, so keep adjusting until you find what works for you and your team.

Celebrating Micro-Wins and Progress to Build Momentum

Momentum doesn't come from big actions; it grows from small wins. This idea isn't just motivational talk; it's based on how your brain works. When you finish even a small task, your brain releases dopamine, which boosts motivation and makes you feel good. That feeling encourages you to keep going, even when things are hard or the goal seems far away. Over time, collecting these small wins helps your brain connect effort with reward. This is how discipline becomes a habit, and habits become second nature.

You can make small wins visible and fun in any setting, whether you're leading a team, working with volunteers, or managing your own goals. In team meetings, try a "win of the week" where everyone shares a recent success, no matter how small. It could be solving a tough tech problem or following up with a difficult client. At home, get creative: keep a "done" list for completed tasks, or put notes about achievements in a victory jar. Read them out loud or pick one at dinner for a quick celebration. Volunteers appreciate playful digital badges like "Follow-Up Pro" or "Shift Saver," or even a simple thank-you meme after a long day. These small gestures cost little but build loyalty and energy.

It's easy to focus on results and neglect the process, but lasting accountability grows when you celebrate effort and consistency, especially under stress or during setbacks. The best recognition is timely and specific, not just generic praise. Instead of saying "Good job," call out what worked: "You kept the team updated even when things got chaotic. That made a huge difference." Or, "I noticed you stuck with your workout plan all week, even after those late nights." When people feel seen for their grit, not just their wins, they're more likely to push through rough patches.

Small celebrations make a big difference during hard times. I've seen teams get stuck, miss deadlines, and lose energy. One group I worked with changed things by starting "progress parties." Every Friday, no matter how far behind they were, the team spent fifteen minutes sharing what had moved forward. It could be clearing old tasks, having a good call, or just making it through the week. The mood shifted from defeat to determination. Momentum returned because people saw that progress was still happening, even if slowly.

Families can use sticker charts to track healthy habits or chores; each sticker marks an effort, not just a final result. When the chart fills up, everyone enjoys a small reward together. It sounds simple, but watching those stickers accumulate motivates both kids and adults. The act of recognition is tangible and shared.

Neuroscience confirms what your gut already knows: progress is power. Every time you acknowledge a step forward, you reinforce the behavior you want more of, whether that's focus at work, kindness at home, or showing up when you'd rather quit. Over time, these bursts of dopamine from micro-wins reshape your habits and identity. You start seeing yourself and your team as people who finish what they start.

To keep celebrations meaningful, make them regular and spontaneous, not forced or over-scheduled. Change who leads recognition so everyone gets a chance; quieter people often notice wins that others miss. For bigger groups, try digital leaderboards that update as tasks are finished, using fun emojis or badges to make progress visible. For yourself, write down one small win each day to create a personal record you can look back on when you need motivation.

A culture of small wins not only boosts morale but also builds resilience. When setbacks happen, people remember their progress and keep going. They learn that effort matters, courage can be seen, and momentum comes from taking one step at a time, even if each step is small.

Creating Continuous Improvement Without Overwhelm Using a Feedback Loop

Feedback gets a bad reputation; many people brace for criticism or expect vague, routine praise that never actually helps them grow. In reality, feedback is the oxygen of progress. Think of it as a loop, not a one-off event. The cycle is simple: observe what happened, reflect honestly on it, adjust your approach, and repeat the process. This loop fuels improvement, not just for individuals but for teams and organizations alike. If you skip any piece, reflection, action, or follow-up, you lose momentum and miss real learning. Feedback isn't about judging performance or fixing people; it's about discovering what works, what doesn't, and what can be done better next time.

A good feedback loop starts with being clear. When giving feedback, focus on specific actions and their results. Don't make it personal or use labels. For example, instead of saying, "You're always late," say, "I noticed you arrived after 9 am three times last week, which delayed our start. How do you see it?" This keeps the conversation based on facts, not assumptions or judgments. If you're getting feedback, listen with curiosity, not defensiveness. Ask questions like, "Can you give me an example?" or "What would you like to see instead?" The goal is to learn, not to argue.

Feedforward is a helpful approach. Instead of focusing on what went wrong, look at how to improve in the future. Ask questions like, "Next time, what would make this easier for you?" or "How could we do this differently?" This encourages new ideas and makes feedback feel like teamwork rather than criticism. It creates space for brainstorming and growth instead of blame.

Building regular feedback rituals keeps things light and prevents overwhelm. You don't need hour-long reviews or formal surveys to create value. At the end of each meeting, spend five minutes on a quick feedback round: "What worked well today? What could we try differently next time?" Make this habit, not an exception. In larger groups or organizations, try a monthly 360-degree reflection, where each person shares one thing they appreciated about others and one thing they'd like help with going forward. These routines lower the stakes and make feedback part of your culture, not just something that happens when there's a problem.

The real benefit comes when you act on feedback and make visible changes. If your team reviews a project and everyone notices communication problems, don't just agree and move on. Assign someone to try new messaging tools or adjust your meetings. Make a plan together, write down the next steps, and check back at the next meeting to see what's changed. For individuals, keep a feedback journal. After each review or tough talk, write down one thing you'll do next time and a deadline to check your progress. This habit turns good intentions into real accountability.

One group of volunteers I worked with struggled with last-minute cancellations and confusion over who was doing what. After gathering candid feedback on the signup process, which many found confusing, they created a new online calendar and began sending reminders 2 days before each shift. The result? Fewer no-shows and more satisfied volunteers. They didn't just gather suggestions; they acted on them fast, then checked back to see if things improved.

Feedback shouldn't feel like just another task. When it's part of your regular routines at work, at home, or with friends, it gets easier and more helpful over time. You stop worrying about being judged and start looking forward to insights that help you improve.

To close this chapter, remember that real improvement comes from steady observation, open conversation, and taking action. The feedback loop is your ally—keep it active, keep it honest, and use it to help yourself and others get better results every day. Next, we'll look at how to maintain accountability even when power dynamics change or when you need to influence without direct authority.

Chapter Six

Scripts for Real Accountability Moments

Bringing Up Missed Deadlines Without Sounding Petty

We've all encountered missed project deadlines, whether a report, a marketing task, or a promised update. Instead of results, there's silence. Addressing this can seem harsh or petty, so accountability conversations often stall. Many avoid direct discussion, leading to frustration or subtle hints. However, addressing missed deadlines is crucial for building trust.

Choose your emotional tone carefully, focus on understanding and forward movement instead of blame. Begin with curiosity and a shared goal, like, "I noticed the report wasn't in by Thursday. Can we talk about what happened?" This approach shows a focus on results and builds trust, making it easier for others to be honest and open.

Concentrate on preserving the relationship and achieving results. Remind them of your shared goal: "I want us both to succeed, so let's get this back on track." This encourages honesty and respect, helping the team feel valued and more open.

Ask open-ended questions to uncover the real reason for the delay. Instead of, "Why was this late?" say, "Was something unclear, or did another priority come up?" This clarifies issues and fosters a sense of partnership, encouraging openness and trust.

Such questions often reveal issues like unclear expectations, increased workload, or poor processes. Once you identify these, resolve them together; maybe urgent requests disrupt priorities, or deadlines aren't visible. Addressing issues early helps resolve problems before they escalate.

Next, create a fair, doable recovery plan together. Involve them instead of imposing deadlines. For example, say, "Let's agree on a new deadline and check-in point." Ask, "What will help you meet the next target?" This boosts their buy-in and shows trust. If they need more time or clarity, work on solutions together.

Use the accountability framework to ensure next steps are clear and specific. This helps readers understand how to apply it for effective follow-up.

Accountability Conversation Checklist

- Open calmly, ask about the missed deadline.

- Reinforce shared purpose ("I want us both to succeed and keep things moving.")

- Ask open-ended questions to find root causes.

- Ask how you can help ("Is there anything I can do differently next time?")

- Co-create a recovery plan ("Let's agree on a new timeline and check-in point.")

- Clarify needs for support ("What would help you meet the next target?")

- End with confidence ("I'm sure we can get this back on track together.")

These accountability framework conversations may feel awkward at first, but repeated use makes them easier. Focus on solutions and cooperation rather than blame. With practice, the framework becomes second nature, enabling the team to quickly and constructively resolve missed deadlines.

Remember, accountability conversations using this framework are not just about fixing mistakes. They also build trust and help teams excel. Addressing issues with curiosity and clarity, core elements of the framework, strengthen shared purpose and real accountability.

How to Address Underperformance with Radical Candor

Radical candor serves as a feedback framework: care personally, challenge directly. This method balances valuing the person and being clear about needed changes. Offering only care is kind but ineffective; the only challenge feels harsh. True radical candor, the framework's goal, expects real effort with genuine concern.

Applying the radical candor framework, address underperformance immediately, specifically, and respectfully. Feedback, when modeled this way, focuses on behavior rather than the person. For example, say, "I've noticed the last two presentations didn't include the data points we agreed on. Can you help me understand what's going on?" This keeps the dialogue honest and constructive.

The radical candor framework relies on avoiding generalizations and focusing instead on specific behaviors and their consequences. For example, say, "In last week's meeting, our client asked about the quarterly numbers, and we didn't have them ready. That made us look unprepared.

What happened there?" This keeps feedback actionable and grounded in the situation, while closely following the framework.

Expect and Manage Emotional Reactions

Be ready for pushback; feedback can trigger frustration or embarrassment. Stay calm and show empathy: "I see this is frustrating." Reassure them: "I intend to help you succeed." Feedback supports growth, not punishment.

Refocus Conversations on Solutions

If the discussion drifts into excuse-making or defensiveness, the radical candor framework instructs you to steer back to solutions. Ask, "What support would help?" or "What would make it easier to meet expectations?" This framework highlights trust and shared problem-solving.

Establish Clear Accountability

After identifying root causes within the radical candor framework, jointly set clear next steps. Ask questions like, "What's a realistic target for improvement over the next two weeks?" Encourage them to define success, then document these commitments. This ensures the framework is actionable and trackable.

Plan for Follow-up

Plan regular check-ins to monitor progress. For example, say, "Let's meet again on Friday to check in." This shows growth matters and keeps everyone accountable.

Practicing Radical Candor

Practicing Radical Candor: Consistently using the radical candor framework strengthens its effectiveness. Even as the balance varies day to day, keep intent and continual improvement at the center. Over time, relying on the framework normalizes feedback as supportive and helpful.

If you're new to radical candor, give feedback soon after issues arise; don't wait. Use facts and observations, not labels. If emotions escalate, pause and return later. This shows respect and keeps things constructive.

Radical candor, as a framework, shifts accountability conversations from criticism to partnership in growth. It encourages results through trust and respect. Over time, the framework helps teams embrace feedback openly and improve together.

Navigating Peer-to-Peer Accountability by Holding Friends, Not Just Reports

Peer-to-peer accountability relies on its own framework: directness combined with humility. It's challenging to hold a peer or friend accountable, so it is important to follow a structure that ensures equality and mutual respect. Real progress requires both trust and a shared accountability framework.

In this framework, peer managers should address issues directly while collaborating. For example, say, "I noticed we both missed the deadline. Can we talk about what's getting in our way?" Reframe problems as shared challenges within this peer accountability structure to make feedback constructive and less personal.

The peer accountability framework recommends finding support-focused solutions together: "How can we keep each other on track without stepping on toes?" Include yourself in commitments, such as "Let's both list our commitments and send a quick update." This approach makes accountability routine and helps clarify shared roles.

Within the peer accountability framework, regular mutual check-ins are most effective. Use tools like calendar invites to make accountability habitual and clear. Keep check-ins brief and focused on priorities and obstacles. The goal is consistent and fair follow-through, not perfection.

When peer accountability conversations become tense, return to the framework of empathy and relationship-building. Say, "I value our partnership and want to make sure we're both set up for success." Invite feedback on your own actions to reinforce shared responsibility and reduce tension within the peer framework.

If things still feel tense after giving feedback, check in privately and gently. You might say, "I noticed things felt tense after we talked about timelines last week. Did I come off too strong?" This gives your peer a chance to clear up any misunderstandings before they grow, and it shows humility and openness. These qualities help build trust and make future conversations easier.

To prevent problems, set ground rules early. Decide together how you'll handle missed commitments, maybe a quick Slack message or a weekly review, what reminders are okay, and how you'll give feedback if things start to slip. Write these agreements down somewhere everyone can see, like a shared document or chat, so no one forgets the plan.

If a peer starts to deflect or blame, gently bring the focus back to your shared goals. You can say, "We both want this project to succeed. I'm hoping we can figure out what's holding us back." Keep the conversation focused on making things better and celebrating shared progress, instead of getting stuck on past mistakes.

Good peer-to-peer accountability is ongoing, not just a one-time talk. Regular check-ins make feedback feel less personal and more about the work you share. It becomes a normal part of your routine, not a criticism. Over time, this habit builds trust, so you can give honest feedback without hurting the relationship. The result is more open conversations, easier feedback, and projects that move ahead with less stress and more energy.

Take a Moment to Consider

Think of a peer or friend at work with whom collaboration sometimes gets sticky. What's one small ritual or check-in you can propose this week to strengthen mutual accountability? Write your script for raising the idea, and imagine the best possible response.

Conversation Blueprints for Volunteer and Community Contexts

Accountability in volunteer and community groups can feel very different. People are there because they care, not because they have to be. There's no paycheck or formal authority, and everyone is balancing other parts of life. Motivation comes from within, and authority is usually shared and informal. If you push too hard, you might lose goodwill or even a valuable volunteer. But if you avoid accountability, projects can stall, and the group's impact can fade. The challenge is to keep everyone working together without sounding bossy.

Picture yourself as a community garden coordinator with a team of volunteers. You see the signup sheet for weekend watering is empty again, and no one has signed up. You need the beds watered, but you also want to keep things positive. The words you use matter. You could say, "I noticed the signup sheet for Saturday is still empty. Can anyone volunteer?" This way, you respect everyone's choice while encouraging action. If tasks are being missed, you might add, "We agreed to water the beds twice a week; is anyone having trouble making that work?" This makes accountability a group issue, not a personal one, and lets people share any problems without feeling blamed.

A good way to maintain strong commitment in these groups is to use inclusive language and to hold regular group check-ins. Instead of blaming or sending lots of reminders, bring everyone together and ask, "Let's talk as a group, what's working well and what's getting in the way?" This opens up honest conversation and helps find hidden problems. People might say they can't do weekday shifts or that the task feels lonely. Once you know the challenges, you can work together on solutions, such as pairing volunteers or planning themed workdays with snacks and music.

Accountability in volunteer groups also grows with creative encouragement and public recognition. Sometimes, just saying thank you at the end of a meeting does more than any reminder. Publicly appreciating someone's extra effort shows that reliability is valued. A "volunteer of the week" mention in an email or at a potluck can build pride and encourage others, without making anyone feel bad. Some groups give small rewards, such as a coffee gift card or letting someone choose the next activity. These gestures aren't about competition; they make reliability something everyone wants to show.

Using visual cues and shared tools can remind people of their commitments without nagging. Keep sign-up sheets in a public place, like a wall or fridge, or in a shared online document, so everyone knows where help is needed. Digital reminders in a group chat, like "Hey team, we're still looking for someone to help with setup on Saturday!" are effective because they reach people where they already talk. Pairing up volunteers or having check-in partners can also help, since people don't want to let each other down.

When things slip through the cracks, and it will happen, avoid guilt trips or sarcasm. Instead, use words that invite people to think about solutions. For example, say, "It looks like we missed watering on Tuesday; what could help us stay on track next week?" or "Is there anything that would make it easier for folks to sign up?" These questions give everyone a say and remind the group that progress depends on everyone's help.

Sometimes you need to reset accountability. If the group's energy drops or people lose interest, have a casual meeting, a pizza night, or a walk in the park to talk openly about what's working and what could be better.

Give everyone a chance to suggest changes. Maybe you adjust the schedule, clarify expectations, or make tasks more flexible during busy times. The goal isn't perfection, it's building good habits while keeping things fun.

Sharing stories about the group's impact can also strengthen commitment. After a successful event or project, share photos, quotes, or short stories that show what was achieved because people followed through. Seeing real results makes future commitments feel important, not just another thing on a busy calendar.

To sum up: use positive language, make invitations open and clear, and recognize people regularly. Use group routines and visual reminders to keep commitments visible without micromanaging. Remember, most people want to do good work; they need help balancing it with their lives and knowing that their effort matters.

Accountability in volunteer and community groups isn't about strict rules or formal consequences. It's about creating an environment where following through feels good, and being involved is something to be proud of. When you find this balance, people come back not out of obligation, but because they feel valued and part of something meaningful.

To wrap up, remember that real accountability grows from each conversation, whether you're leading a team, working with peers, or organizing volunteers. How you talk about follow-through affects how people respond and how your group works together. In the next chapter, we'll look at how to keep accountability strong when things get stressful or change quickly, so your systems stay solid even when life gets tough.

Chapter Seven

Managing Up, Down, and Sideways forAccountability Without Authority

Managing Up to Hold Senior Staff Accountable When You Lack Power

Getting the input you need from someone higher up can be tough. Imagine being a mid-level manager, stuck waiting for a VP's approval. Reminders and deadline alerts haven't worked, and now your team is stalled. Each day without a decision hurts your credibility. You don't want to come across as difficult by pushing too hard, but silence doesn't help your team or the business.

Managing up isn't easy. Senior leaders decide on promotions and budgets, setting the tone for the workplace. You might worry about upsetting them or being seen as too demanding. It's helpful to understand common objections or resistance you may face, so you can prepare responses that keep the conversation productive. This awareness helps you navigate challenges without damaging relationships or credibility.

So, what can you do? Remember, holding senior staff accountable isn't about confrontation or calling them out. It's about working together on shared goals and making hidden obstacles clear. Be diplomatic, respectful, but direct. Executives pay attention to facts and business impact, not emotions. When you bring up an issue, focus on real consequences and deadlines. For example, say, "When we don't get feedback by Friday, the project slips a week, risking client satisfaction," instead of just saying, "We're waiting on your feedback." This helps your audience feel more confident that their efforts are aligned and valued, encouraging cooperation.

Being diplomatic matters. Don't blame or use a passive-aggressive tone. Instead, use language that shows you want to work together. For example, instead of saying, "You missed the deadline," try, "What's the best way to keep you updated on blockers so approvals aren't delayed?" or, "How can I make it easier for you to provide what we need on time?" This shows respect for their role, clarifies your needs, and reassures your audience that you intend to support mutual success, fostering a sense of partnership rather than conflict.

Make it easy for executives to act. Share information briefly and clearly, using bold text or visual timelines, and always link your request to business value. For example: "If we finalize this decision by Tuesday, we'll launch on time and avoid extra costs." Keep requests short and specific; clarity reassures your audience that their actions will lead to positive results, reducing frustration and encouraging prompt responses.

Even when you do everything right, you might still get silence or pushback. In these situations, you may need to escalate, but always do so professionally. To escalate effectively, first document all your requests and conversations. Next, clearly explain why escalation is necessary and what you hope to achieve. Then, involve a neutral party, such as the project management office or a trusted colleague, to underscore the urgency.

Finally, ensure your escalation is based on business needs, not personal frustration.

An Escalation Toolkit Using an Email Template & Reflection

Escalation Email Template:
Subject: Decision Needed by [Date] to Avoid [Impact]

Hi [Leader's Name],
Our team is waiting on [specific approval/feedback] to move forward with [project/task]. If we don't decide by [date], we risk [impact: delay, lost revenue, missed deadline]. Is there anything I can do to help move this along? I'm happy to coordinate or provide more info if helpful.

Thanks for your attention. I want to keep us on track for our goals.

Best,
[Your Name]

Let's take a moment to consider

Think of a situation where you're awaiting input from above. Write out how you'd frame your ask in terms of data and impact, not frustration, and draft an escalation message using the template above.

If escalation doesn't work, widen your support network. Involve a credible peer or cross-functional leader who shares your goals. Say, "I've copied [Project Manager] since this affects both our timelines. Hoping we can align quickly." Allies with leadership credibility strengthen your message.

For example, I worked with a product team that was stuck because the C-suite hadn't given clear direction. The team lead tracked every missed milestone and the expected financial impact in a visual dashboard. Sharing this as a straightforward update at a leadership meeting, not as criticism, helped executives see how their delays were affecting the business. After that, bottlenecks cleared, and regular check-ins were scheduled.

Stay persistent but not aggressive. Keep issues visible and stick to the facts, not personal feelings. This approach turns potential confrontations into shared accountability.

Managing up benefits the entire organization, not just you or your team. Use clear communication, support your requests with data, and always offer solutions to build trust and credibility. Start today: identify one area where you can raise an issue using these strategies, and take action to hold yourself accountable. By acting professionally and standing up for what matters, your influence and your team's results will grow.

Lateral Moves for Cross-Functional Accountability in Matrixed Teams

Working with other teams can feel like juggling different priorities. Marketing wants a campaign ready by Friday, but the product is still testing features. Customer service has open questions, and project management asks for updates that don't match what's really happening. In cross-functional teams, accountability is often unclear. Unlike traditional teams, boundaries are blurry, and responsibility can be confusing. Not knowing "who owns what" often leads to missed deadlines, confusion, and finger-pointing that hurts trust.

At a typical launch meeting, marketing and product may both assume the other is handling key tasks. The issue isn't skill or effort, but unclear ownership. Each group focuses on its own goals, which can conflict. Without clear goals, you might end up with a great campaign for a product that isn't ready, or a finished feature that no one is promoting. When priorities aren't clear, accountability drops, and teams spend more time sorting things out than progressing.

To avoid confusion, set clear expectations before the project gets going. Begin joint projects with a kickoff meeting to clear up any assumptions.

Bring everyone together and explain the project's purpose, what success looks like, and why it matters to each person. Use a simple checklist: What's the main goal? Who's responsible for each part? What are the deadlines? Where will decisions be recorded? Who needs to be consulted, and who needs updates? Writing this down helps everyone know what's expected.

Visual tools like swim lane diagrams are very helpful. They show who is responsible for what at each stage of the project. When everyone can see these responsibilities, it's harder for anyone to say they didn't know their role. Swim lanes also help spot bottlenecks early, so teams can adjust before work slows down. Shared project boards or real-time Google Sheets also keep everyone updated and make progress clear.

Even with good planning, teams sometimes clash. Marketing may need a demo video for an unfinished feature, or teams may define "go-live" differently. When this happens, keep conversations open and blame-free. After milestones, hold joint retrospectives. Ask, "What went well?" and "Where did confusion arise?" This encourages honest feedback and solves issues early.

A neutral facilitator, such as an HR partner or someone not involved in the project, can help keep tough discussions on track and ensure everyone, even quieter team members, is heard. Focus on the facts, like missed handoffs or gaps in communication, and work together to find solutions. Aim to fix the process, not blame people.

Track team commitments using shared dashboards to clarify deadlines and deliverables. This transparency helps spot problems early so you can get support before they become urgent, not to assign blame.

Peer-to-peer accountability is important. Hold regular meetings, not just for updates but also to highlight risks and ask for help. Rotate who leads these meetings to avoid power struggles and encourage everyone to take ownership. Try peer-review demo days to catch problems early and give feedback.

Let each department take turns sharing status updates. This keeps teams engaged, ensures everyone feels valued and responsible, and prevents anyone from missing their chance to report.

Working across teams is rarely straightforward. Priorities can change, new obstacles can pop up, and people might lose sight of the project's main goal. That's why regular, short check-ins are important. A 15-minute weekly meeting focused on deliverables, blockers, and upcoming decisions can help keep everyone aligned.

To boost accountability right away, try drawing your project as a swimlane chart. List functions like marketing, product, and operations across the top, and steps down the side. Draw lines to show where responsibilities overlap or are handed off. Then, meet with your team to review the chart and fill any gaps in ownership, turning what you learn into clear actions.

Building trust between departments with different priorities isn't easy. But setting expectations early, making ownership clear, tracking progress openly, and having honest conversations help teams work together smoothly and achieve lasting results.

Influence Over Authority Using Scripts for "Managing Without the Title"

If you've ever wondered how to motivate others without having a formal title, you're not alone. Maybe you're new in your career, a specialist, or part of a large team, and you see what needs to be done but don't have a "boss" badge. The good news is that real influence isn't about job titles. The people who drive accountability best are those who build trust, form good relationships, and let their work speak for itself. Teams start to rely on you not because you enforce rules, but because you're consistent, clear, and helpful. When you deliver updates, solve problems, and keep everyone informed, you become the go-to person, even if your title doesn't require it.

You build informal influence by being reliable and having a strong track record. When you come prepared, share information openly, and keep your promises, people trust you. Colleagues know they can count on you; if you say something will be done by Friday, it gets done on time. This trust is valuable and lets you help shape how work gets done, even without formal authority. When someone needs an update or help connecting teams, be the one who steps up, offers help, or makes introductions. You don't have to know everything, just be helpful when it matters and give credit to others.

The words you use can help bring people together around shared goals. Since you can't give orders without authority, invite others to join in: "I'd love your input on hitting this target, what do you think?" This shows you respect their experience and value their ideas. When you need support, show what you're doing first: "Here's what I'm doing, could you handle X?" People are more willing to help when you lead by example. These approaches aren't manipulative; they create a sense of partnership.

It can be hard to pitch ideas when you don't have authority, but how you present them makes a difference. Instead of announcing decisions, start a conversation: "I've been thinking about improving our process. Do you see any gaps we should address?" Getting others involved in problem-solving helps them buy in. If someone seems unsure, ask: "Does anything in this plan give you pause?" This shows you're open to feedback and helps people feel more comfortable.

Accountability works best when it's visible. Use social proof. After meetings, ask everyone to share what they're responsible for: "Let's each share what we're taking on and check in next week." Saying commitments out loud in front of others helps people follow through. This isn't about shaming, it's about making progress clear and shared. Tools like Slack can help by highlighting wins: "Great job to Alex for those quick edits!" These shout-outs motivate people and encourage good habits.

Making progress visible to the group helps everyone stay accountable. Use shared documents or dashboards to track progress. People like seeing their work recognized. Celebrate small wins to build momentum. In larger teams, try a regular "Wins & Next Steps" section of meetings, where everyone shares what they finished and their next priority. This keeps everyone focused and makes follow-through a normal part of the process.

When change feels risky or new processes seem overwhelming, informal networks can help. Find a trusted team member to try new behaviors with you. Ask them privately, "Would you try this accountability ritual with me for a month? If it works, we can share the results." Starting small makes it easier for people to give new things a chance.

Pilot projects are very useful. Get a few volunteers to try out new routines, like check-in meetings, group trackers, or peer reviews. Share updates about what's working. After a few rounds, highlight successes: "Our pilot cut missed deadlines in half after two weeks!" Share these results with other teams to build interest and show that the system works.

Working together gets more done than going it alone. To build accountability across teams or up the chain, partner with colleagues who also see the value. A small group can track progress, share lessons learned, and build excitement as results become evident, such as fewer missed tasks, faster feedback, and greater consistency.

If you ever feel overlooked or undervalued because you don't have a big title, remember that influence comes from trust and getting results, not from hierarchy. When people count on you for honest updates, encouragement, and shared wins, they'll look to you no matter your position. Your impact is built on reliability and results, not job titles.

Building Influence Without Authority

List three colleagues who could help your project move forward: peers, cross-team partners, or respected informal leaders. For each, note a recent win or helpful action they've taken. Reach out this week: thank them authentically and invite them into your next step, like, "I'd love your input on making this smoother, what do you think?" Track responses and shifts in the dynamic.

Momentum grows through shared goals and regular recognition, built one conversation at a time.

Getting Buy-In from Skeptics and the "That Won't Work Here" Crowd

Resistance happens in every workplace. Sometimes it's a sigh in a meeting or someone saying, "Here we go again," when a new accountability process is announced. You'll spot the skeptics; they might cross their arms or look distant, often because they've seen too many failed initiatives. Their doubts aren't just about laziness. Usually, it's frustration, disappointment, or even fear. Think of someone who's seen leaders introduce new dashboards or "big ideas" that disappear after a few months. Over time, people get tired of change, and even good ideas are met with, "We tried that before." Deep down, people worry about being micromanaged, losing control, or being judged for mistakes.

Objections come in many forms. Some people worry about slowing down: "Won't all these check-ins slow us down?" Others fear losing independence: "I do my job well, I don't need extra oversight." Some are just tired: "We've managed this long without it, so why change now?" These concerns are real. No one likes wasted effort or feeling watched. To make progress, you can't just push through these concerns; you need to understand their origins and respect people's experiences.

Listening with empathy is your best tool. Instead of jumping into your pitch or defending your plan, start by asking questions and showing real interest. For example, say, "I hear you think this could slow us down. Can you share an example from before?" This helps people feel heard and gives you useful information about past problems. Sometimes you'll hear about systems that created too much paperwork or leaders who used data to single people out. When you ask, "What's worked for you in the past for follow-through?" you invite people to share their own solutions. Often, they'll mention routines or tools that already help, which you can build on.

Addressing objections directly doesn't mean giving in. It's about working together to find a better solution and showing you're not forcing a one-size-fits-all fix. If someone worries your new tracker means more work every Friday, you could ask, "Would it help if updates were every two weeks? Or should we try a quick team huddle instead?" Being flexible helps turn skeptics into partners. If someone says they're too busy at the end of the month, suggest moving deadlines or letting them try a simpler version first.

Persuasion isn't just about having the best argument; it's about using the right approach for your audience. Some people respond to stories. If you have an example of a team that improved with accountability rituals, like a sales team that started hitting targets after weekly check-ins, share that story. Show the before-and-after: missed deadlines and confusion turned into clear wins and less blame. Others want data. Share numbers from pilot projects: "We saw on-time delivery improve by 30% after starting short daily standups." For those who are still unsure, suggest trying it as an experiment: "Let's try this for two weeks and see how it goes. If it doesn't help, we can change or stop."

Trying things out in small steps works well for teams that are nervous or have had bad experiences before. Present it as an experiment: "We'll test this for a sprint, then get everyone's feedback." Making it low-pressure helps people feel safer about joining in. When people see their feedback shapes what stays and what goes, they become less resistant.

Quick wins help change people's minds. If one person or team benefits early, like hitting every deadline for a month after starting check-ins, highlight that success. Thank them publicly, share their story at the next all-hands meeting, and ask them to explain what changed. Testimonials from team members are powerful because people trust their peers more than outside promises.

Build momentum by celebrating small successes. You could set up an online "wall of wins" where teams post achievements and thank each other for help. Highlight early adopters by focusing on results, not just effort: "Shout out to Support for clearing their backlog after trying our new review process." This makes the new behavior normal and encourages others to try it too.

Some workplaces value independence or tradition, so not everyone will join in right away. Let positive peer pressure build naturally. When people see real benefits, like less confusion, smoother handoffs, and fewer crises, they'll become curious and may want to join in themselves.

In summary, getting buy-in isn't about forcing people or winning arguments. It's about respecting doubts, inviting honest feedback, and making room for small experiments and visible wins. When you meet skepticism with empathy and flexibility, people start to see accountability as something they're part of, not something forced on them.

As you think about building personal accountability outside of work, remember these lessons: trust grows through shared successes and honest conversations, not from top-down orders. In the next chapter, we'll look at how these ideas can help you create habits and systems that match your values, even when no one else is watching.

Chapter Eight

Overcoming Resistance by Turning Objections into Opportunity

Dispelling the Myth That Accountability Is Not Micromanagement

Many people feel uneasy with frequent manager check-ins or sudden progress reviews. Leaders often struggle to balance offering support with being seen as micromanagers. This confusion can erode trust and morale. The key message: accountability and micromanagement are not the same.

Accountability relies on trust and respect. It involves clear agreements on responsibilities, deadlines, and success while letting people decide how to work. When you lead with accountability, you allow team members to use their judgment. In contrast, micromanagement involves controlling details and constant oversight, stifling initiative, and making people doubt their value. Actions may appear similar, but accountability helps people grow while micromanagement breeds frustration.

Why does this myth persist? Many leaders mistakenly equate involvement with control, especially in important moments. Extra oversight may feel safe, but it often signals distrust. Constant monitoring shows a lack of faith, causing even top performers to lose interest. Check-ins meant to help can backfire if they seem more like policing than support.

To change this pattern, leaders and team members need to be clear and open. Rather than asking for constant updates, set expectations from the start: "Here's what needs to be done and by when. You choose how to get there." Support independence with words like: "Check-ins are here to help, not to watch over you. I'm here to support, not to get in the way." This kind of language respects people's skills and builds their confidence.

If your team still feels that any follow-up is micromanaging, address it openly. Say, "I trust how you work, so let's focus on results during our check-ins. If you run into problems, let's talk about how I can help, not control." When someone meets their commitments, recognize it: "You did this your way; the results speak for themselves." This kind of recognition encourages responsibility instead of making people feel watched.

Accountability vs. Micromanagement Self-Check

Reflect on your last two team projects or commitments:

- Did you (or your leader) set clear expectations for outcomes and deadlines?

- How much freedom existed in choosing how to reach those results?

- Were check-ins framed as support or inspections?

- Did updates leave you or others feeling motivated or stifled?

Looking at these details helps you see whether your approach encourages accountability or risks becoming micromanagement.

Real change comes when teams move from micromanagement to accountability. For example, a creative director used to request daily status updates on design elements. Her designers soon did only the minimum, stopped suggesting new ideas, and felt stifled. After receiving feedback, she replaced daily pings with weekly outcome reviews that focused on the deliverables. The team regained ownership, started volunteering ideas, and deadlines improved because they now felt trusted.

Similarly, a software engineering team suffered from low morale as their manager constantly checked Slack for updates on every ticket. This led to resentment and stalled productivity. After an honest discussion and review, he switched to biweekly milestone meetings focused on results and roadblocks, rather than micromanaging every step. Morale rebounded, and the team began exceeding goals.

In summary, fostering accountability through clear agreements and supportive check-ins yields trust and creativity; micromanagement rarely delivers results. But what if your culture is proudly casual or creativity-driven? For these environments, accountability can still thrive if you tailor it to fit.

Making Accountability Work in Laid-Back and Creative Cultures

If you've heard, "We're too relaxed for that," you're not alone. Startup and creative teams value flexibility but get frustrated when projects stall or go off track. The core lesson: even relaxed cultures need clear accountability that fits their style. Flexibility and structure can coexist to boost both creativity and reliability.

In teams where "let's see what happens" is common, chaos can take over. I've seen smart startups lose momentum because no one tracks responsibilities. Wanting freedom often leads to confusion, missed deadlines, and repeated problems. Adding some structure, like Monday meetings or Friday "show-and-tell" sessions, creates a routine that supports independence. These habits aren't about control; they set a pace for everyone to do their best.

To build accountability in creative teams, choose routines that respect everyone's style. For example, creative groups use "Demo Days," where people show progress however they like by Friday, keeping results visible. Another idea is to set "minimum viable commitments," the smallest steps that move a project forward each week. Instead of a strict checklist, the team might agree, "Let's each finish one thing by Thursday." These small promises keep things moving without draining the team's energy.

Accountability works best when the team creates the rules together. Start a brainstorm with the question, "What does accountability look like for us?" Some may want Slack reminders, others sticky notes, or even check-ins over coffee. Share ideas and write group agreements: "We'll use chat for reminders, check in every Monday, and if someone needs more time, just say so." Accountability becomes something everyone owns, not just a rule from the top.

Real teams prove this works every day. There's a design agency I know that starts each week with a fifteen-minute kickoff, everyone shares their top priority, and ends with a Friday "show-and-tell." It's fast, fun, and the creative director never judges style or format. The result? Fewer dropped balls and more energy at the finish line. In another example, a music collective wanted more consistency but hated meetings. They invented rotating "commitment buddies," pairing up each week to check in on each other's progress; one text midweek was all it took. Suddenly, more tracks got finished, and nobody felt micromanaged.

Build-Your-Own Accountability Ritual

Grab your team (or even just your project partner) for a five-minute brainstorm:

- What's one ritual we could start doing to see progress every week?

- How do we want to remind each other—text, chat, sticky notes?

- What's the smallest commitment each person can make by next Friday?

Write down your answers and try them for two weeks. Adjust as needed; this is about finding what works, not perfection.

You don't have to pick between freedom and structure. When accountability aligns with your team's values and style, creativity takes off. People know what's expected, but can still work their own way. That's how unique teams deliver bold ideas and keep their energy." Tried That Already": Diagnosing and Fixing Past Failures

When you hear, "We tried that already," it usually comes from failed attempts at accountability. Leaders introduce new systems that fade quickly. The core problem: lack of clarity and follow-through. Without clear expectations and leadership, people give up, doubting that anything will last.

Another problem is making things too complicated. Too many forms, confusing tracking, and another problem is making things too complicated. Too many forms, confusing workflows, and a lack of follow-through can make simple tasks feel like a chore. I've seen teams try new systems for weeks, only to have leaders revert to old habits. Burnout isn't just about too much work; it's about effort wasted on changes that never last. When people say, "Nothing ever sticks here," you know the cycle is deep. Meet with your team and ask, "What worked before? Where did things go wrong? What was missing?" Be specific. Was the process unclear? Were expectations vague? Did tracking tools make things confusing? Was feedback missing, or was the system just too complicated? Anonymous surveys can help people share honest answers. Sometimes parts of old systems worked—maybe regular check-ins built trust, but the tracking tools were too much. Or maybe people lost interest because leaders didn't follow through.

Once you know what didn't work, restart accountability with openness and humility. Don't ignore past failures; talk about them. Say, "Here's what we tried, here's what didn't work, how can we improve?" Let everyone help design the new process: "What would help you stay on track? How do you want reminders or recognition?" Involving people from the beginning uses their ideas and builds ownership. If you're a manager, admit where you made mistakes. Being open encourages others to be honest, too.

After restarting, momentum comes from quick, visible wins. Find small steps everyone can take in the first week to make early success likely. This could be logging one update, sharing a problem in your chat, or reaching a simple milestone. Track these wins in meetings or on a shared board. Celebrate all progress: "Three people posted updates this week, great job!" Share stories from team members who notice positive changes. These examples help convince skeptics that things are different now.

"What Was Missing?"

Set aside 10 minutes with your team (or on your own). List three failed accountability efforts. For each, jot down: What worked? What didn't? What was missing? Then ask: If we could try again, what would we change first? Use these notes as a guide for a fresh approach.

You don't need to be perfect at the beginning. What matters is honest feedback, clear commitment, and being willing to adjust. As small wins add up and people see their input making a difference, even skeptics start to believe change can happen. That's how you go from "We tried that already" to "This time, we made it work."

When People Resist Accountability, Try Navigating Pushback

Resistance to accountability usually comes from something deeper than laziness or stubbornness. I've seen people push back for reasons that have little to do with the process itself. Fear of being judged, past embarrassment, or the belief that the system isn't fair can all cause hesitation. Sometimes people worry about being singled out in front of others. Employees don't want to be called out in meetings, and volunteers may fear that speaking up means getting stuck with more work. These feelings are real and come from real experiences. When handled poorly, accountability can feel like a trap rather than a way to grow.

When you encounter resistance, your first reaction might be to push harder or argue. But that usually makes things worse. People get defensive and dig in. Instead, it's better to listen and try to understand what's behind the pushback. If someone says, "This feels unfair," or "I'm worried I'll get blamed," pause and say, "I hear your concern. Can you tell me more about what's behind that?" This question opens up an honest conversation rather than a power struggle. Often, the real issue is fear of embarrassment or a bad experience with a past manager who used accountability to shame people. In these moments, showing empathy is more important than making your case. Edge off by inviting people to help shape the process. Ask, "What would make this feel fair and supportive to you?" Give them space to suggest ways of checking progress that don't trigger anxiety. Some may prefer private check-ins over public updates; others might want to choose how often they report progress. The trick is not to surrender standards, but to show flexibility in how they are met. For example, let teams pick their own check-in cadence, maybe one group thrives with weekly updates, while another prefers a quick chat every two weeks. Honor that difference as long as commitments don't slip.

Having a few scripts ready can help when things get tense. I often say, "My goal is for everyone to succeed. What's getting in your way?" or, "Are there parts of this process that feel like too much? What could we change?" These questions do more than calm people down; they help you find real problems. Sometimes people feel overwhelmed by too many tasks or worry that missing a commitment once will be held against them. By bringing up these concerns, you can adjust the system so it works for everyone.

Transforming resistance into real engagement takes time, but it can happen. I remember a team member who always rolled his eyes when we talked about accountability; he'd had bosses who used it to punish rather than support. After a private talk, he chose his own approach to tracking progress, using a simple checklist he shared only with me. His attitude changed. Within two months, he met his commitments and even started helping others stay on track. He became an accountability buddy for new hires, a big change from his earlier skepticism. They face an even trickier challenge. When people fear they'll be stuck with all the work if they speak up, retention plummets. I worked with a local community group struggling with this very issue. Instead of assigning tasks outright or holding people accountable in public meetings, we switched to an opt-in ritual: each volunteer chose their commitment for the next event and could adjust up or down each time, no hard feelings, no shaming. Suddenly, participation jumped, and more people returned month after month, because they felt safe managing their involvement on their own terms.

Resistance isn't an obstacle to steamrolling; it's a signal to slow down and ask questions. By listening to concerns without judging and changing how you practice accountability, not what it means, you can turn skeptics into supporters. Accountability becomes something people want to join rather than avoid. Often, the loudest critics become your biggest supporters when they feel heard and have real choices in how they take part.

Accountability is harder when you work with volunteers or in groups without formal leaders. You can't rely on titles or paychecks to make sure people follow through. People join for different reasons; some want to help, others want to meet friends, and some have free time. High turnover is common. You can't enforce rules like in a regular workplace. Instead, you need flexibility, a shared purpose, and lots of positive feedback to keep people coming back and doing their part.

Volunteer coordinators know this challenge well. Sometimes you have plenty of helpers, and other times you're scrambling to fill spots. The first step is to reconnect everyone to the mission. People need to know their work matters. Reminding the group of its purpose at every meeting isn't just a habit; it's what keeps people motivated. It helps everyone remember why they joined and shows even the busiest volunteer how their efforts fit into the bigger picture. When you focus on the mission, like "We're here to make sure every family has a meal tonight," or "Our park cleanup keeps our town beautiful," you inspire people's hearts, not just their hands.

Peer accountability is very effective in these nontraditional groups. Group agreements set the tone; it's about shared expectations, not top-down rules. Your team might start meetings by reading a short mission statement or spend a few minutes deciding who's responsible for what that day. Recognition is just as important. A quick "shout-out" for someone who arrived early or stayed late encourages the right behaviors. Instead of waiting for the leader to praise, let peers recognize one another. This builds momentum and shows everyone's efforts matter.

Plug-and-play rituals make accountability feel less like management and more like community. Rotating task lists on a whiteboard lets everyone see what needs to be done and who's on deck. When roles change each week, nobody feels stuck or singled out. Simple text reminders before events cut down on no-shows; they're low-pressure but keep commitments visible. Another helpful tool is a "commitment circle" at the start of each shift: volunteers gather briefly, share what they're focused on, and voice any needs or concerns. These circles foster ownership and signal that everyone is part of the team, not just filling a slot.

Tracking in these groups should be as simple as possible. Whiteboards, sticky notes, or a group chat work well. Making things too complicated will quickly turn people off. The important thing is that commitments are easy to see and update, so no one gets left out.

Recognition should be creative and genuine. "Volunteer of the Month" awards work well, print a photo, write a few lines about what the person did, and display it where everyone can see. Celebrate group milestones with pizza nights, potlucks, or simple thank-you circles after big events. Sometimes, a personal thank-you note from a leader or someone helped by the project means more than any prize. These small gestures of gratitude make people want to come back.

Low-stakes consequences are important too. If someone misses a shift, they might take on an extra task next time or help clean up after an event. It's about keeping things fair, not about punishment. The main thing is to avoid shame and focus on helping everyone contribute again.

Building accountability in these groups is about creating a culture where everyone feels noticed and connected to the mission. People come back when they know their role, feel recognized, and see that their time matters.

As you use these ideas, shared mission, clear commitments, and real recognition, you'll see your team become more reliable and motivated, even without formal authority. The next step is learning how to rebuild trust when things go wrong and keep moving forward after setbacks. That's where real resilience begins, and that's what we'll cover next.

Chapter Nine

Personal Accountability Playbook That Goes Beyond the Workplace

Building Self-Accountability with or Without a Boss

It's late Wednesday. You're alone at the table, laptop open, coffee cold. No boss, just your deadline. That freedom can become a trap. You plan to finish a proposal before lunch, but lunch drifts into an afternoon online, and the deadline is pushed to tomorrow. Freelancers, remote workers, and solo entrepreneurs face this as well. When you answer only to yourself, flexibility can turn into avoidance.

Take Jamie, a freelancer. She planned to launch a website, pitch clients weekly, and keep up with invoices. Without check-ins, her launch was delayed from March to May, then stalled. She worked long hours but often missed critical tasks. This is common. Without pressure, it's easy to procrastinate and feel guilty. Remote workers lack regular oversight, so small tasks crowd out big goals. Solo business owners stay busy but may not finish what matters.

Accountability needs more than good intentions; it needs a clear process. Use a weekly self-review: What did you promise? What did you do? What did you meet or miss? Write your answers. Seeing progress and setbacks can boost your confidence and motivate you to stay on track. If you keep putting off tasks, ask yourself why. Is it difficult or unclear? Would smaller steps help? This habit makes actions specific and trackable.

Add pressure with public commitment. Share your goal with someone, a friend, partner, or group chat. Saying, "I'll send this pitch by 3 pm," makes follow-through more likely, since someone else knows. Public commitments can foster a sense of pride and connection, encouraging you to follow through because you want to uphold your reputation and feel part of a community.

If you lack someone to share goals with, create accountability through artificial deadlines and consequences. Try: "If I don't send my invoice by Thursday, I'll donate $20 to a disliked cause." Or, owe a friend coffee or do an extra chore if you miss a deadline. Small consequences can inspire a sense of responsibility and motivate action when motivation is low. Time-blocking helps too: schedule tasks as appointments and only reschedule if necessary.

Celebrate consistency. After finishing an important task, reward yourself by ordering takeout or by enjoying a walk with music. Small rewards reinforce good habits. If you slip or miss a goal, reflect with kindness. Ask: What got in the way? Was my goal realistic? What can I change? Focus on learning and adapting, not criticism. Over time, accountability becomes part of who you are, even after setbacks.

Weekly Solo Accountability Checklist

- What did I promise myself this week?

- What did I fully complete?

- Where did I fall short, and why?

- What got in my way (distractions, unclear steps, outside demands)?

- What's one change to try next week?

Each week, write your answers in a notebook or digital file. Review past weeks to spot patterns. Regular reflection keeps you focused and reveals what motivates follow-through.

Using solo systems means you don't rely only on willpower; you build momentum, even alone. These techniques complement other accountability types, forming a solid foundation. People who stick to goals often have a secret: accountability to someone else. An accountability partner is more than a friend; they check your follow-through, even when no one else notices. Social motivation is strong. If someone expects an update, you're less likely to delay. Accountability partners help you move from "I'll do it later" to action.

Choosing the right accountability partner is key. Not every friend or coworker fits. Pick someone reliable who keeps promises and endures tough times. Avoid those who make excuses or let you off the hook. Good communication matters. Choose a listener who gives honest, helpful feedback. Ideally, your partner shares your goals or understands them. Ask: Do I trust this person's privacy? Are they honest but kind? Will they hold me accountable? If not, keep looking for a better fit.

Once you choose your partner, set clear rules: how often to check in and what counts as a win or a slip. Some like daily texts, others weekly calls, or shared online docs. Set clear expectations. Will you give direct feedback, even if it's hard? What if someone misses a commitment? For example: "We text on Monday and Friday, each share a goal, and report progress. Miss a check-in? Reschedule within 24 hours." Write the agreement.

Keep your check-ins short, clear, and focused. A simple "three-bullet update" works well: What did I accomplish? Where did I struggle? What's my next step?

Shared documents or spreadsheets can help both partners track progress. Some people like using voice memos for a more personal touch. Choose whatever keeps you committed, but make sure it doesn't get so casual that you forget to follow through.

If the partnership loses momentum or someone misses check-ins, address it quickly but kindly. Say, "Our check-ins are slipping. Can we tighten up?" If excuses appear, reset: "Let's talk about what's not working and improve." If that fails, changing partners can bring new energy. The aim is honest effort and real progress, not perfection.

Feedback can feel awkward, especially if your partner struggles. Keep it supportive and solution-focused: "I noticed you're stuck, want to brainstorm ways to make it easier?" Be direct but caring to avoid guilt or resentment. Remember, you started this partnership for honesty, trust, and shared growth. Real change comes from shared responsibility, not just stating goals.

Personal Habit Trackers Are Tools

Tracking habits clarifies intentions. You may plan to work out or eat healthier, but plans fade without a record. Track your actions, even just a checkmark. This ends wishful thinking and builds evidence. Marking a box or swiping gives satisfaction. These wins add up and help fight procrastination. Progress, even slow, makes habits hard to ignore.

Habit tracking's psychological principles are simple but powerful. We like to finish things. When you check off a task, your brain gets a reward, making you want to repeat it. A habit tracker highlights progress and encourages you to keep going. Over time, you link behavior to success, making habits stick.

Pick a tracker based on your style and routine. Digital tools work if you're always on your phone. Apps like Habitica, Streaks, or Loop Habit Tracker help you set up habits, track progress, and add fun with rewards or reminders. Habitica gamifies habits; Streaks is simple and visual; Loop is good for Android with flexible tracking and data exports. Digital tools are portable and send reminders before motivation fades.

Analog trackers have their own benefits. Writing things down with pen and paper can feel more real than using a screen. Bullet journals let you customize as much as you want; you can draw boxes, use colors, or add doodles for milestones. Wall charts or sticker calendars make your progress easy to see, and each sticker feels like a small reward. For families or roommates, a shared wall chart in the kitchen can create friendly competition and help everyone stay honest. The best thing about physical trackers is that they're always visible, no app to open or password to remember, just clear accountability.

To set up a habit tracker that really helps, make it personal and simple. Start with no more than three habits; any more can feel overwhelming. Write them out clearly, like "Drink two liters of water," "Walk 20 minutes," or "Read before bed." Decide how often you'll track them. Daily works best for most habits, but some might be weekly, like "Call Mom on Sundays." Create a monthly template and leave space to note how you felt, what got in your way, or why you succeeded. Try using colors, red for important habits, blue for mood-related ones. This helps you spot patterns, like noticing that stress makes it harder to exercise but doesn't affect your reading habit.

Almost everyone has trouble tracking habits at some point. You might forget for a few days, feel discouraged after missing a streak, or fall into "all or nothing" thinking, where one missed day feels like failure and makes you want to quit. Instead of giving up, try a habit restart: circle the missed days, write "restart," and treat each week as a new beginning. When you feel overwhelmed, focus on micro-habits. If a "30-minute workout" seems too much, aim to put on your sneakers. Any progress counts, no matter how small.

Use A Monthly Habit Tracker

At the end of the month, look for streaks and celebrate them, circle any five-day run of a habit, and count it as a win. If you see gaps, don't ignore them; they're just feedback, not something to judge. Mixing structure with flexibility helps you keep going, even on tough days. Tracking should be about honest progress, not perfection.

Reset Rituals To Break Out of Accountability Fatigue

Accountability fatigue can creep in when you're running on empty, stuck in a cycle of missed commitments, or so overwhelmed by your to-do list that you freeze. This mental exhaustion builds up after weeks or months of trying to stay on track, telling yourself you'll do better tomorrow, only to find your motivation gone. You might notice guilt outweighing your progress, your calendar filling with tasks you dread, and each day ending with a feeling of falling behind. You may start avoiding certain projects, making excuses, or feeling numb even when you finish something. When this happens, accountability feels like stress rather than growth.

To get out of this rut, pause and permit yourself to reset. Start with an "accountability audit." Take a notebook or open a blank document. List all your current commitments, work, family, side projects, and self-improvement goals. For each one, ask yourself: Does this help me move forward, or is it just weighing me down? If a commitment no longer helps you, or you're keeping it only out of habit or guilt, cross it off or postpone it. For anything you keep, write down why it matters to you now. This audit isn't about quitting; it's about clearing your mind and regaining focus.

Create a weekend reset ritual. Set aside an hour on Saturday or Sunday when you're less busy. Start by sitting somewhere comfortable and quietly reflecting on your week. Think about the highlights, the things you avoided, and what drained your energy. Write down your thoughts without editing. Then, plan: What are your top three priorities for next week? What's one small reward you'll give yourself for sticking to them? It could be a favorite meal, a walk in the park, or an hour without your phone. Connect your planning to something that helps you feel refreshed rather than weighed down.

Guilt can become harmful if you don't address it. That's why it's important to practice forgiveness and recommitment when you feel fatigued by accountability. Try this five-minute self-forgiveness exercise: Find a quiet place, close your eyes, and say or write, "I forgive myself for dropping the ball. I am learning, not failing. I release today's guilt so I can start again tomorrow." Take a slow breath as you let go of self-criticism. To help create a fresh mindset, try writing a "fresh start" letter to yourself. Start with "Dear Me," and honestly acknowledge any recent struggles, but be gentle. Then write what you want to believe about yourself going forward: "I am capable of change. I will focus on progress, not perfection." This isn't just a symbolic act; it helps change your internal story from one of shame to one of possibility.

To avoid future fatigue, add proactive strategies to your routine before you get overwhelmed. Plan regular "no-accountability" days, 24 hours when you don't track habits, chase goals, or check off lists. Give yourself a break and notice how your motivation returns when you have some space. Change up your goals every few weeks to keep things interesting. If you've been working on one project for a long time, switch to something new or lighter for a while. Add variety to your habits by trying a new walking route, cooking a different dish, or listening to new music during your routines. Mixing things up keeps your mind engaged and makes it easier to stay consistent.

Remember: accountability should feel like support, not punishment. Build in short breaks between cycles of effort, mini-vacations from responsibility where you reconnect with what excites you outside of checklists and deadlines. When you sense burnout creeping in again, don't ignore it; use these reset rituals as early warning systems that help you recalibrate before you lose momentum completely. Treat resets as a natural part of growth, not as evidence of failure. Accountability is sustainable when it breathes; you don't have to be relentless every single day to stay true to yourself.

Aligning Daily Actions with Your Deeper Values

If you feel off track or keep procrastinating, it's usually not because you're lazy or bad at managing time. More often, the real problem is that your daily actions don't match what you truly value. Even if you work hard and reach your goals, you might feel empty if your efforts don't fit with your core beliefs. This can lead to a frustration that's hard to explain. That's why you might keep putting off certain projects, not because they're difficult, but because they don't matter to you or don't fit with who you are.

Figuring out your values isn't just a theoretical exercise; it's a practical step toward lasting accountability. If you don't know what matters most to you, it's easy to get caught up in being busy, say yes to everything, and end up feeling drained. To get clear, make a list of what's important to you, like health, honesty, family, creativity, adventure, stability, learning, or connection. Don't overthink it, write. Then, choose your top five. Which values make you proud, or would you defend in an argument? This list will help guide your future decisions.

Turn your values into clear, daily actions. It's not enough to say you value kindness if your schedule leaves you stressed and irritable. Make each value concrete. If health is important, take small steps, like taking the stairs, packing your lunch, or stretching before bed. If connection matters, call a sibling every Sunday or message an old friend each week. When your values show up in your actions, accountability becomes real.

Regularly check whether your actions align with your values through self-audits. Look at your calendar and to-do list, do they reflect your priorities or someone else's? Each week, ask yourself what you did to honor your core values. Did you support a friend or learn a new skill? Record these actions in a journal or habit tracker so they stand out. Over time, this helps you notice when you're living in line with your values and when you're not.

When you're clear about your values, it's much easier to say no. You stop feeling guilty for stepping away from things that don't fit, and start feeling proud for protecting your time and energy. Turning down a project or stepping back from an obligation takes courage, but it's freeing. You can use phrases like "Thanks for thinking of me, but this isn't the right fit," or "I'm prioritizing other commitments right now" to set boundaries. These words aren't selfish, they're responsible.

Living by your values doesn't mean you never compromise or always get it right. Sometimes work or family will pull you off track. The goal isn't perfect alignment, but regular reflection and adjustment. Use your values to guide new opportunities and to check in when you feel frustrated or restless. When things feel off, ask yourself: Am I acting in line with what matters most? If not, what small change can I make today?

In the end, accountability is about more than just getting things done. It's about making sure your actions bring you closer to the life you want. When your actions match your values, motivation comes more naturally, and you feel more satisfied. You trade guilt for clarity and regret for progress.

To sum up, grounding your accountability in your personal values helps you act with purpose and avoid distractions. It's not always easy, but it leads to more fulfillment and self-respect. Next, we'll look at how these habits can spread, changing not just your life but also the culture around you.

Chapter Ten

Repair and Recovery For Rebuilding Trust After Letdowns

The Anatomy of an Effective Apology and Course Correction

Picture yourself facing someone whose trust you've lost, a colleague, employee, teammate, or your child. You know you've let them down and can sense their disappointment. Just saying "I'm sorry" doesn't feel like enough. How you respond now will affect your relationship going forward. Most people have been in this situation, but few know how to apologize in a way that truly rebuilds trust. Many apologies only make the speaker feel better. It's tempting to make excuses, use vague words, or say "I didn't mean to." But genuine repair requires honesty and humility, which are essential for rebuilding trust effectively.

Start by stating what happened without downplaying it: "I missed the deadline for our quarterly report," or "I promised to be home early and wasn't." Being clear shows respect and maturity. Then, describe the impact: "Because I missed the deadline, your team had less time to review the numbers," or "You had to wait for dinner and probably felt unimportant." This demonstrates that you understand their feelings, which helps the audience feel more connected and empathetic.

Taking responsibility is where many apologies fall short. Don't use phrases that avoid ownership, like "I'm sorry if you felt..." or "Sorry things got messed up." Instead, own what you did: "I didn't deliver what I promised," or "I dropped the ball." Being honest like this is key to trust. Next, show how you'll fix things with specific actions: offer a new timeline, explain your next steps, and set a follow-up. For example: "I will submit the revised report by Friday noon, review the process to avoid future delays, and check in with you on Monday to ensure the solution works." This clarity demonstrates your commitment to rebuilding trust through concrete actions.

Your tone and words should always match the relationship and situation. For managers who miss a promise, admitting mistakes can feel risky, yet it is essential for credibility. For example: "I told you I'd get feedback on your proposal by Wednesday and failed to deliver. You counted on me, and my delay made your work harder. This was my error. My new plan: I'll send detailed feedback by tomorrow noon and set calendar reminders in the future. Let me know if you need anything else to get back on track." This approach stays direct and reassures the audience that you are committed to transparency and improvement.

When working with peers, where there is no hierarchy, being genuine is especially important: "I didn't upload my part last night as agreed. That left you scrambling on your own, which was unfair. This was my oversight. I'll handle any last-minute edits, and next week I'll submit my work ahead of time." This shows you own the mistake while avoiding defensiveness.

At home, parents may be tempted to blame missed promises on being busy, but showing accountability teaches resilience: "I said we'd go to the park after dinner, but work calls kept me. That was disappointing, and I should have managed my time better. To make it up, let's schedule it for Saturday morning so nothing else interferes."

Most apologies go wrong not because of bad intentions, but because people don't realize their words sound defensive or make the problem seem smaller. Avoid phrases like "I'm sorry if you felt upset," which blame the other person's feelings. Also, avoid "Mistakes were made," which avoids taking responsibility. These kinds of phrases make people doubt your sincerity. Instead, be direct: "I'm sorry I didn't follow through." It's simple, honest, and shows you're taking responsibility. It takes more than just words; you need to act. Remember, an apology is only the first step. After you apologize, lay out what you'll do next: set a follow-up ("Let's touch base next Friday to check my progress"). If needed, make a clear plan, adjust deadlines, or keep everyone updated. This shows you're serious and builds trust.

Your Apology Blueprint

Think of a recent time when your apology didn't cover everything. Rewrite it using these four steps:

- Say exactly what happened;

- Describe its impact;

- Fully accept responsibility;

- Explain how you'll fix it.

Notice how this feels compared to just saying "sorry." If you can, try giving this new apology in real life or practice it with someone you trust.

Following up, keeping your new promises, and asking for feedback show that your apology is more than just words; it's a real effort to rebuild trust and confidence. These steps are even more important if you've let someone down more than once, since it takes more work to earn back trust. Consistent actions and open communication are key to restoring credibility over time.

A Step-by-Step Approach To Rebuilding Trust After Repeated Letdowns

When trust is damaged, it doesn't come back just because you want it to. Suppose you've let someone down more than once, you'll start to notice a "trust deficit" in how people treat you. Maybe a colleague avoids eye contact or stops volunteering to work with you. They might leave you out of new projects or quietly double-check your work. This isn't just in your head. It's a real sign that people are skeptical. After several missed deadlines or broken promises, people pull back. You might get fewer invitations, less feedback, and a sense that expectations are lower. This trust gap is real. It hurts both morale and results.

After repeated letdowns, words alone won't fix things. You can't just say, "I'll do better next time," and expect people to trust you. Now, people need proof, not promises. If you're in this situation, maybe after missing team deadlines or not showing up for volunteer work, the way back starts with being completely open. First, admit that trust is broken. Show you understand why others are cautious. You don't need to beg for forgiveness, but you should acknowledge the tension. Next, focus on "under-promising and over-delivering." Take on small, simple tasks and finish them every time. Don't jump into big projects yet. Instead, show up consistently. Let your actions rebuild trust.

Being transparent isn't just about saying what you'll do. It's about showing your progress. Start tracking your tasks where everyone can see them, even if it feels uncomfortable at first. For example, send weekly emails to your team listing what you promised and what you finished. Use shared checklists or a whiteboard if you're in the office. Make your progress clear to everyone. Don't wait for someone to ask if you finished a task. Update them first: "This week I finished X, Y, and Z as promised." If you run into problems (and you will sometimes), let people know early. Say, "I'm having trouble with X, here's what I'm doing to fix it and my new timeline." This openness might feel like too much, but it's what's needed when trust is low.

You build reliability by consistently meeting small goals. Don't try to make up for lost trust with one big gesture. Focus instead on small wins: for instance, send out an agenda before every meeting for a month, or always arrive on time. People notice patterns, not just one-time efforts. Each time you deliver on a promise, you move people from doubt to trust. Also, ask others to check in on your progress or review your updates. This isn't about approval. It shows you're open to feedback and willing to be accountable.

Real team stories show how this process works in practice. I once worked with a project coordinator who missed several key handoffs during a product launch. This caused problems and frustration across teams. She admitted her mistakes and asked her manager to give her only low-risk tasks for a few months. She tracked her work in a shared document and sent short weekly updates about what she finished and any problems she faced. As she built a strong track record, she was gradually given bigger projects again. It took almost six months of steady work before her teammates started seeking her input without hesitation. For example, I watched a senior leader mishandle a major company project, leading to many employees working late on weekends and confusion about changing goals. Instead of making excuses or hiding behind his position, he set up a public dashboard to track his goals and improve communication and project clarity. Every week, he shared his progress at all-hands meetings and asked his team for honest feedback on how he could improve. He followed through by setting clearer agendas, sending recaps within 24 hours, and checking in one-on-one with anyone affected. Over time, as people saw real changes, complaints faded.

Regaining trust isn't a straight path. There will be setbacks, missed goals, or old doubts after a mistake. But steady, consistent action builds credibility over time. The most important thing is to keep your commitments visible and let others hold you accountable. This creates shared ownership. People feel safe trusting you again because they can see your progress and speak up if needed. rust, you need to give people time and space to believe in you again at their own pace. Show you're reliable through repeated actions, so doubt turns into confidence, not because you said so, but because they saw it for themselves. If you're patient and let your actions speak for themselves, opportunities will return. Trust rebuilt this way is often stronger, shaped by honesty, humility, and a promise to rely on actions rather than just words.

Turning Mistakes into Team Learning Moments

Mistakes will happen, but how you handle them shapes your team's future. Too often, when things go wrong, people look for someone to blame, ignore the mistake, or move on. But if you treat every mistake as a chance to improve not just yourself but the whole team, you build something better than a perfect record. One of the best ways to turn mistakes into progress is to make learning from them a team habit, not a source of shame.

When something goes wrong, like a failed campaign or a project that didn't work out, bring your team together for a blameless review. The goal isn't to find out who "messed up," but to see what happened, where things broke down, and what everyone can learn. Start with honesty: "We missed our target. Let's figure out what went wrong, together." Focus on systems, communication gaps, and process issues, not personal mistakes. For example, after a marketing campaign fails, ask: Did we define our audience clearly? Were deadlines realistic? Was feedback shared in time? This way, people feel safe to speak up, knowing the goal is to improve, not to punish.

Having a repeatable process for these reviews keeps them useful. I like the "What, So What, Now What?" model. First, ask people to describe what actually happened, without guessing or adding details. Next, talk about why it matters: What were the effects on the team, clients, or company? Finally, decide on next steps: What should we do differently next time? This structure keeps the conversation focused and practical. If your team struggles to be open, try collecting lessons learned anonymously using digital forms or sticky notes. This can bring out honest feedback that might not come up in person.

As a leader or facilitator, sharing your own mistakes sets the example. When you talk openly about a decision that didn't work out, like underestimating how long a project would take or misjudging a client's needs, you show that it's okay to be vulnerable. In my experience, saying "I missed something here" helps others drop their guard and think about their own actions without fear. This isn't about beating yourself up, but about showing humility and a real desire to learn. When leaders admit their mistakes in meetings, team members are more likely to speak up early or admit confusion before small problems become big ones.

Making it a habit to talk about mistakes helps build this mindset. Try adding a "failure of the week" discussion to your regular meetings. This isn't about blaming anyone, but about saying, "Here's what didn't go as planned, and what we learned." These talks can be short, but over time, they help everyone see that setbacks are chances to learn. Another good habit is to keep a team learning log or a digital wiki. After each project, write down what worked, what didn't, and any patterns you notice. This record helps inform future decisions and lets new team members learn from past experiences, rather than repeating mistakes.

Monthly brainstorming sessions can also keep learning going. Set aside time each month for everyone to suggest improvements or flag ongoing problems, such as unclear meeting agendas, slow software, or communication gaps. Try out small changes from these sessions and review how they worked at the next meeting. Over time, this builds a habit of consistently seeking ways to improve, rather than just reacting to problems.

Team Debrief Checklist

For your next project debrief or post-mortem, use this checklist:

- Did we clarify what actually happened?

- Did everyone get to share their view?

- Did we focus on processes and systems instead of blaming individuals?

- What did we learn that surprised us?

- What will we do differently next time?

- Did we document our insights somewhere accessible for future reference?

When you make these habits and tools part of your team's culture, mistakes become chances for everyone to grow, not just sources of stress. Teams that learn openly bounce back faster from setbacks and become more resilient and creative over time. Each mistake adds to your shared knowledge, making future successes more likely and failures less intimidating. In this kind of environment, people feel safe taking smart risks and know that, even when things go wrong, something useful will come from it.

Creating a Culture Where It's Safe to "Fail-Forward"

You might hear the phrase "fail-forward" in business or self-help talks, but what does it really mean? At its heart, failing forward means seeing mistakes as steps forward, not dead ends. In high-trust, high-accountability teams, failure isn't ignored or used to blame people. Instead, it's seen as a chance to try new things, take smart risks, and build resilience. The difference between failing forward and just failing again and again is what you do after a mistake. Failing forward means reflecting, learning, and making real changes. Failing over and over is just repeating the same mistake without learning from it.

A clear sign you're in a place that supports failing forward is how early and openly people talk about risks. In teams with psychological safety, employees point out problems before they get worse. Someone might say, "I'm running behind on this task," or "I'm not sure this approach will work." Instead of hiding issues, people bring them up because they trust mistakes won't be held against them. After a mistake, team members suggest ways to improve instead of making excuses or blaming others. They focus on fixing the process, not just the symptoms. It's normal to hear questions like, "What could we try differently next time?" or "How can we make sure this doesn't happen again?" These behaviors show you're in a safe and supportive environment.

Building this kind of culture takes effort. Leaders, official or not, play a big part. If you want your team to talk about mistakes and learn from them, you need to reward openness and effort, not just perfect results. This could mean giving a shout-out at a meeting to someone who admitted a problem early or thanking someone who suggested a review after a mistake. You can even create informal awards, like a "learning badge" or a small trophy, for team members who try new things, even if everything doesn't work out.

Recognizing honesty in this way shows that being open is just as important as success. If your team only hears praise for perfect work, people will start hiding anything that looks like a weakness. But if you openly appreciate those who bring up problems or suggest improvements, you show that growth matters more than looking good. Over time, this encourages everyone to share real challenges, leading to quicker problem-solving and more creative ideas.

You can take real steps to build a fail-forward mindset in your organization. Start by holding pre-mortem meetings before big projects, gather your team, and ask what could go wrong and how you'd handle it. This simple habit uncovers hidden risks and makes it normal to discuss potential failures in advance. After projects finish, hold post-mortem meetings focused on lessons learned, not just on what went right or wrong. Make sure these meetings are safe spaces with clear rules: no blame, no shaming, just honest reflection.

Leaders can also show fail-forward thinking by sharing their own weekly reflections on what didn't go as planned. When someone in charge says, "Here's what I tried last week that didn't work, and here's what I'm doing differently," it sends a strong message. It shows everyone that mistakes are normal and that real professionalism is about how you adapt.

Another good idea is to set up "safe space" forums or open-door hours where anyone can talk about setbacks without worrying about gossip or consequences. These could be regular lunch meetings, online channels, or even anonymous suggestion boxes, whatever works for your team. The goal is to give people a way to be honest about challenges without risking their reputation.

The words you use every day matter too. Instead of asking, "Who messed up?" try, "What can we learn from this?" Swap "Don't let this happen again" for "What support do you need to succeed next time?" These small changes in language help create a culture focused on progress rather than perfection.

When you make these habits part of your team's culture, you get more than just fewer mistakes; you get innovation. People try new things because they know mistakes are part of learning, not career-ending. They bounce back from setbacks quickly because they feel supported and able to solve problems rather than hide them.

In short, creating a culture where it's safe to fail forward means moving from perfectionism to progress, from fear to curiosity, and from blame to shared growth. The best way to improve over time is through steady experimentation and honest talks about what went wrong and why. As you move forward, keep this mindset in mind: lasting change and accountability depend on your willingness to learn openly and adapt before problems become crises.

Chapter Eleven

Accountability as a Community to Sustain Change for the Long Haul

Rituals and Rhythms for Making Accountability a Shared Practice

Think of a time you belonged to something bigger, a team, family, or volunteer group. What made it special was not just the shared goals but the shared purpose and actions: Monday huddles to share wins and worries, Sunday dinners to plan the week. These rituals turn accountability into action by adding structure, predictability, and a sense of belonging. They keep expectations grounded in real experiences.

Rituals set a steady pace and provide regular opportunities to build trust and reinforce commitment. For example, when your team meets every Friday for a quick action review, you check in face-to-face on progress, which helps everyone stay on track and feel supported. At home, a Sunday planning session lets all voices be heard and strengthens family bonds.

These are more than meetings; they're reminders of what matters, who counts on whom, and how everyone is moving forward together. In teams I've worked with, these recurring circles act as the group's heartbeat, keeping everyone accountable not through guilt, but through shared purpose and trust. Family check-ins, even with young kids, help build pride in following through and in learning from one another.

To make rituals effective, include everyone in their design, so each member not only feels involved but also clearly understands how the ritual supports accountability. Rituals don't have to be elaborate; even simple, repeated actions like check-ins can lay the foundation for group responsibility. Try asking your group, "What kind of check-in would help us most?" When teams pick their review days or rotate facilitators, engagement increases and shared ownership grows. For example, a commitment jar makes each person's progress visible and gives the group a concrete way to support one another. The greatest benefit is turning accountability into a supportive, shared process that encourages progress rather than blame.

You don't have to stick with boring routines. Customizing rituals to suit your group-whether a team, family, or volunteer group-makes them more meaningful and enhances accountability and motivation. Try a quick commitment round during meetings for updates, light a candle to mark completed promises in volunteer groups, or use digital streak badges for tech-savvy teams. Families can keep a whiteboard tally for chores or goals. The most important aspect is that the ritual fits the group and feels natural, as rituals that resonate with the group's style are more likely to build lasting accountability.

Even the best rituals can lose impact if they become stale. To sustain their benefits, regularly update rituals to align with what motivates your group. Leaders can bring in new ideas or gather feedback to keep rituals relevant and effective, such as adding recognition programs or music. Establish simple ways to measure success, like tracking participation or mood, so you can see what's working. If enthusiasm fades, see it as a sign to refresh your approach. Continuous renewal ensures that rituals maintain their power to support accountability and keep everyone engaged. With rituals and rhythms in place, the next step is creating the physical and digital tools your group will use for ongoing support.

Design Your Own Ritual

Grab a notebook or open a doc and brainstorm with your group:

- What time feels right for regular check-ins?

- How can you mark completed commitments, stickers, high-fives, and tally marks?

- Who wants to lead next week's meeting or family session?

- What's one small tweak you'd like to try?

Vote on your top choices and commit to testing your new ritual for two weeks. Afterward, check in on how it felt, what brought energy, what fell flat, and adjust as needed.

Rituals aren't about strict routines or perfection. They offer reliable opportunities to build accountability into daily life. By repeating practices together, even simple ones, you make both expectations and progress visible, which strengthens trust, connection, and lasting commitment. Over time, shared rituals turn accountability into a natural habit that benefits everyone in the group.

The Accountability Lab for Building Your Own Toolkit and Community

See your accountability lab as a place to build and refine tools that help your group put plans into action. Pick what fits your group's style; whether it's meeting checklists in your workspace or a digital dashboard for tracking progress. These tools should simplify things, make achievements and setbacks easy to spot, and be adjusted together until they fit. After you have a toolkit started, you can also strengthen accountability through community resources and peer interaction.

You can take this further by sharing what works both within and beyond your group. Create a shared folder with templates, meeting agendas, check-in prompts, feedback forms, and motivational memes. Allow members to swap their own versions. Consider quarterly tool-swap sessions where people demo their favorite apps or charts, leaving with new ideas. If possible, invite other departments or friends; sometimes an outsider's tool or habit can spark innovation in your group.

Building an accountability community can be simple. Gather a few peers and set up monthly meetups to share resources and encourage follow-through. To keep engagement high, vary activities, celebrate successes, and periodically invite new members. Meetings don't have to be formal; the value is sharing honestly what works. For daily support, create a group chat for updates, celebrations, and help requests. Over time, this space becomes a vital source of ongoing support and encouragement, helping your group stay accountable and connected.

Your toolkit is never "done." What helped last year might not work now. As needs shift, schedule an annual toolkit audit where everyone reviews what's still useful and what's not. Encourage honest feedback and adapt accordingly. Sometimes, inviting outside voices, such as a guest expert or someone from another context, can introduce helpful new ideas and keep your lab energized.

Accountability Toolkit Builder

Try this exercise: set aside 20 minutes with your group. Make a list of every tool you currently use for accountability, digital trackers, sticky notes, scripts, group chats, anything that helps commitments stick. Rate each on usefulness from 1–5. Next, have each person suggest one tool they'd like to add or update this quarter. Pick one idea to test together for the next 30 days. At the end of the month, check in: did it help? Keep what works; ditch what doesn't.

An accountability lab builds community through shared effort and continual improvement. People work together to form routines and test new follow-through strategies. When everyone helps choose and refine tools and shares stories about what does or doesn't work, the toolkit evolves to fit the group.

Peer Support and "Above the Line" Communities Are What Works

Peer support is often key to lasting accountability. It's the feeling when someone is watching, cheering you on, and keeping you honest. Structured support builds reliability. Assigning random accountability partners mixes perspectives and prevents favoritism. You explain your progress not to a boss, but to a peer who also wants to improve.

Above-the-line communities reward taking responsibility, not blaming. Imagine a visible wall or channel where people share moments of stepping up, celebrating action, and growth. Monthly, recognize someone who gives feedback or admits a hard truth. The focus is on rewarding courage to speak up and improve. Using phrases like "That's above the line" helps everyone support each other positively.

Starting a peer accountability group is simplest with 4–8 people for diverse, manageable participation. Rotate who leads and meet biweekly for a quick "wins and stucks" roundtable. Each person shares one success and one challenge, while others listen and help. Sessions should feel like a huddle, not a formal review.

To keep groups healthy, watch for negativity. If meetings turn into complaints, remind everyone that the goal is support and solutions. If energy drops, refresh membership or structure. Sometimes, simply changing location or meeting style helps.

When group habits start to slip or commitment drops, don't ignore it. Speak up directly, for example: "I've noticed our check-ins aren't as lively. Are we still finding them helpful? What could make them better?" Give everyone a chance to share honestly, then work together on a new plan. This might mean changing meeting times, adjusting the format, or even taking a break to reset. The goal isn't to blame anyone, but to invite new commitment and keep the space open for honest conversation. Peer support works because it adapts to everyone's needs and changes over time. When managed well, these communities build accountability through trust and respect, not fear or competition.

Measuring Progress Using KPIs for Teams, Families, and Yourself

You notice a real difference as soon as you start measuring what matters. Tracking your progress with the right metrics isn't about chasing numbers. It's about making your growth visible, so you can see clearly where you're improving and where you're stuck. The key is to pick KPIs (Key Performance Indicator) that actually matter to your group, not just use generic stats from a book or old meeting. For a team, this could be as simple as "percentage of commitments completed on time." Everyone knows the goal, and the number tells a clear story: we're delivering, or we're not. In a family, a KPI might be "number of shared meals with everyone present." Instead of just hoping for more connection, you're counting it and making it real. For yourself, maybe it's "days I went to bed on time" or "tasks I finished that matched my top priorities." The right KPI should encourage the behavior you want, not just show what's missing.

Tracking and showing these numbers turns them from background noise into something that drives action. For teams, putting a dashboard on the screen at the start of each meeting makes accountability clear for everyone. When people see the completion rate for last week's promises, it becomes a shared responsibility. At home, a progress chart on the fridge, with stickers for family dinners or checkmarks for bedtime routines, makes goals real and visible. Volunteer groups can use an "impact meter" on their website to track hours or donations. You don't need fancy software; even a whiteboard or a piece of paper on the wall can make a big difference. Make your metrics easy to update and hard to miss. When numbers are visible where people gather, they start conversations and keep everyone focused.

KPIs work best when they start conversations, not just keep score. A monthly "KPI review" isn't about praise or blame. It's time to ask, "What patterns do we see? Are we moving in the right direction? What's one thing we could try to improve this number?" These talks help people learn and solve problems rather than blame each other. For families, checking the meal chart might spark new ideas, such as changing dinner times or sharing cooking duties. In teams, if on-time completion drops, it can spark a discussion about workload or deadlines rather than silent frustration. The data becomes a starting point for improvement, not a tool for criticism.

I've seen groups change just by measuring what matters and sharing the results openly. One nonprofit I worked with struggled for months to increase attendance at events. When they started tracking RSVP responses and actual attendance each week, patterns became clear: reminders sent three days before events worked best, while last-minute texts didn't help much. Changing their approach based on this data led to full rooms and more energy. In another example, a family tired of messy bedtimes started marking off nights when everyone followed the routine. It wasn't perfect right away, but seeing the checkmarks add up built momentum and even got reluctant kids excited for more streaks. A tech team that had trouble meeting deadlines began posting their "commitment completion rate" at every Monday meeting. The first few weeks were tough, with low numbers, but no one wanted to stay there. Over time, making progress visible and working together helped them improve until hitting targets became the norm.

Making progress visible and useful with KPIs isn't about being perfect or competing. It's about having clarity, so you can celebrate wins, spot problems early, and keep moving toward what matters most to your group. When you use data to start conversations and let people see their progress together, accountability feels less like a burden and more like something you share with pride.

Becoming a Role Model Through Leading Accountability by Example

If you want to change a group's culture, what you do matters most, both when people are watching and when they aren't. Showing ownership consistently has a ripple effect that spreads quickly, whether you're leading a team, supporting your family, or volunteering. People notice how you handle your own commitments. They see if you show up on time, keep promises, and respond when things go wrong. Actions, especially the small daily ones, matter more than words. I remember a manager who stood before the whole team after missing a major deadline. Instead of making excuses, she admitted her mistake, explained the impact, and shared her plan to fix it. That moment changed everything. Suddenly, everyone saw that owning up to mistakes was not just allowed but expected. Trust in the group grew almost overnight.

To model accountability in daily life, focus on small, steady actions. Always follow through on promises, even if they seem minor. If you say you'll send an email, make a call, or bring snacks to a meeting, do it and let others see you did. Being reliable in small things helps others trust you with bigger ones. In meetings or check-ins, give feedback honestly and humbly, and ask for feedback yourself. Say things like, "Is there anything I could do better?" or "What am I missing?" This invites real conversation and shows you're open to learning. When someone else steps up, admits a mistake, or helps out without being asked, recognize it in front of the group. Celebrate these moments openly. It's not about big gestures, but about creating a space where ownership is seen and valued.

Everyone makes mistakes, even those who try hardest to set a good example. What matters is how you handle them. If you miss a deadline or drop the ball, don't hide it. Say directly, "I missed my commitment this week." Then explain your plan to fix it and what you'll do differently next time. This isn't just about fixing problems; it's about showing others how to learn from setbacks. Ask your group to hold you accountable, too. Say, "Check in with me next week to make sure I'm back on track." Being open like this breaks down barriers and builds real trust. People learn that accountability isn't about being perfect; it's about coming back and trying again after a mistake.

Sometimes your biggest impact is helping others become accountability leaders. Notice the people who quietly lead by example, always deliver, encourage others, or help their peers through tough situations. Let them know you see their efforts: "You're great at following through and helping others step up. Would you like to help coach someone else?" Pair new members with these accountability champions so good habits spread naturally. Make space for people to share their stories, and hold informal "leadership story" sessions where members talk about how they handled tough situations or bounced back from setbacks. These sessions aren't about putting anyone above others; they're about building shared growth and learning from each other's real experiences.

Every day, your actions, more than any slogan or policy, set the real rules about what matters. People will match your level of ownership and honesty, even if you don't realize it. When you keep showing up, correcting yourself, and encouraging others to lead, you start changes that can shift the whole culture over time.

As we finish this chapter, remember that leading by example doesn't mean being perfect. It means being visible, consistent, and humble. When you show accountability in both big and small ways, others notice and follow your lead. This is how strong communities are built, not by top-down rules, but by everyday actions that encourage everyone to do their best. In the next chapter, we'll look at ways to keep that momentum going, even when things change or motivation drops.

Conclusion

You made it. If you're reading this, you've truly changed your approach to accountability. When I started this book, my goal was clear: help you stop procrastinating, build lasting habits, and close the gap between your goals and actions. I never aimed for perfection, just freedom from guilt, broken promises, and confusion about what matters.

Looking back, you've come far. We began by confronting a common problem: most equate accountability with blame, finger-pointing, or endless reviews. But you learned otherwise. True accountability is ownership, stepping up, not hiding. Trust in yourself and others makes ownership possible.

You faced challenges like self-doubt, feeling like a victim, and the thought, "Maybe I'm not disciplined." You learned self-trust through small wins, honoring promises, and honest reflection. You practiced learning from setbacks and turning them into lessons.

Next, you built systems, not overwhelming ones, but simple routines that help you follow through. You set expectations, checked in, tracked progress, and made changes as needed. You learned to have tough conversations, whether nudging a teammate, giving your boss feedback, or holding a friend accountable without damage.

You learned to track habits, celebrate wins, and create positive pressure by making your progress visible. You saw how community, rituals, shared check-ins, and group agreements make accountability stick. Together, we faced skeptics and those worried about micromanagement. Now, you handle pushback with empathy and flexibility.

You've built a toolkit. You know how to rebuild trust after mistakes and when your team struggles. You've practiced turning mistakes into learning and shifting from blame to growth. Now, you see accountability as an ongoing team effort.

Let's be clear: Accountability isn't about punishment or control. It's about trust, starting with yourself. It means clarity, knowing what matters, why it does, and who is responsible. It's about consistency, checking in, and making changes before things fail. It's about honest, sometimes uncomfortable conversations focused on learning and growth for your team and community.

Here's what you have now:

- Frameworks for self-accountability, so you manage time, energy, and promises without burnout.

- Systems for team and peer accountability, ensuring everyone knows roles and feels supported.

- Scripts for tough conversations, address missed deadlines or resistance without drama.

- Tools for habit tracking, so you see progress and stay honest when busy.

- Strategies for repairing trust and learning from setbacks turn mistakes into steps forward.

- Rituals and templates for building a culture where accountability is positive, visible, and lasting.

Be proud. Most people stall or get discouraged by failure. You kept going. You gained practical skills and faced yourself, saying, "I'm ready to own this." That's not easy, but it's how everything starts.

Here's my challenge: don't wait. Try one strategy today. Do a five-minute weekly check-in, start a habit tracker, or have that honest conversation you've put off. Action matters more than intention. The first step is the hardest and most important.

Remember, accountability isn't one-and-done. It's ongoing. Use the templates, scripts, and toolkits in this book. Return to the "accountability lab" when things get tough. Improve your systems. Outgrow some tools, keep what works, and let yourself grow.

You don't have to do this alone. Accountability works best with others. If you haven't, join the support group or online forum for readers. Share wins, struggles, and lessons. Ask for feedback, offer insights, and celebrate progress. Resources are there for you, but real magic comes from connection.

Accountability is a daily choice. Progress, not perfection, matters. You can be a role model of consistency, trust, and growth for your team, family, and community. The world needs fewer excuses and more people who show up and own it.

Take action today. See what happens. I'll be cheering you on every step.

More people may also benefit from the information in this book. However, they need your help. If you found this book worthwhile and informative, please leave an honest review in order to help others. Thank you. — George Munson

References

Atomic Habits: Tiny changes, Remarkable results by James Clear. (2026, January 21). James Clear. https://jamesclear.com/atomic-habits

Bloome, J. (2025a, March 12). *How to develop a strong accountability culture in your organization.* Culture Partners. https://culturepartners.com/insights/how-to-develop-a-strong-accountability-culture-in-your-organization/

Bloome, J. (2025b, April 23). *Top Strategies from an Accountability Workshop to Boost Team Performance.* Culture Partners. https://culturepartners.com/insights/top-strategies-from-an-accountability-workshop-to-boost-team-performance/

Browning, H. (2025, May 8). *Yes, you can increase accountable leadership.* CCL. https://www.ccl.org/articles/leading-effectively-articles/yes-you-can-increase-accountability/

Burkus, D. (2025, January 29). How to rebuild trust on a team | David Burkus. *David Burkus.* https://davidburkus.com/2022/05/how-to-rebuild-trust-on-a-team/

Comcare. (2025, December 19). *Building trust in your team.* Comcare. https://www.comcare.gov.au/safe-healthy-work/healthy-workplace/good-work-design/building-trust-in-your-team

Delizonna, L. (2017, August 24). *High-Performing Teams Need Psychological Safety: Here's How to Create It*. Harvard Business Review. https://hbr.org/2017/08/high-performing-teams-need-psychological-saf ety-heres-how-to-create-it

Downer, K. (2022, May 10). *Team Rituals: 35 pretty good ideas to strengthen your culture*. RapidStart Leadership. https://www.rapidstartleadership.com/team-rituals/

Eby, K. (2024, August 5). Free action item templates. *Smartsheet*. https://www.smartsheet.com/content/action-items-templates?srsltid=Af mBOopDqw8vS2EobtDICtVUkdVw6FSM91OiYNV1rJwW5wj8xyeV S9en

Education, R. &. P. (2024, February 13). *Accountability Partners: Don't achieve your goals alone!* Recreation & Physical Education. https://recreation.duke.edu/story/accountability-partners-dont-achieve-y our-goals-alone/#:~:text=Above%20all%2C%20trust%20your%20instinc ts,each%20other%20reach%20your%20goals.

Foley, J. (2025, July 29). *The Fail Forward stories: Share, Grow, Unite | Agile Alliance*. Agile Alliance | Promoting a More Effective, Humane, and Sustainable Way of Working. https://agilealliance.org/resources/experience-reports/the-fail-forward-st ories-share-grow-unite/

Google re:Work - Guides: Understand team effectiveness. (n.d.). Rework. https://rework.withgoogle.com/intl/en/guides/understanding-team-effe ctiveness

Habit tracking methods - Which one is for you? (n.d.). https://www.habitify.me/blog/habit-tracking-methods-which-one-how- to-track-habit

Kane, B. (2026, March 5). *What to do when your brain is too tired to think straight*. Todoist Inspiration Hub. https://www.todoist.com/inspiration/mental-fatigue

Lattimer, C. (2025, October 6). *Building trust in relationships and yourself.* People Development Magazine. https://peopledevelopmentmagazine.com/2024/10/21/building-trust/

Leadership Accountability: Why it matters and how to fuel it. (n.d.). Betterworks. https://www.betterworks.com/magazine/accountability-in-leadership/

Paul, M., & Paul, M. (2016, August 16). *Moving from Blame to Accountability.* The Systems Thinker. https://thesystemsthinker.com/moving-from-blame-to-accountability/

Psychological Safety – Amy C. Edmondson. (n.d.). https://amycedmondson.com/psychological-safety/

Slack. (n.d.). *Team Check-in template and examples for businesses.* Slack. https://slack.com/templates/team-support

Staff, F. R. (2025, April 15). *A Tactical Guide to Managing Up: 30 Tips from the Smartest People We Know.* First Round. https://review.firstround.com/a-tactical-guide-to-managing-up-30-tips-from-the-smartest-people-we-know/

TalentQ. (2022, January 14). *8 simple rituals that build a stronger culture.* https://www.talent-quarterly.com/8-simple-rituals-that-build-a-stronger-culture/

The power of small wins. (2011, May 1). Harvard Business Review. https://hbr.org/2011/05/the-power-of-small-wins

The Table Group. (n.d.). *Peer-to-Peer Accountability: the Game changer | The Table Group.* https://www.tablegroup.com/peer-to-peer-accountability-the-game-changer/?srsltid=AfmBOor9ZnO8KbKg0_j0DgyMFXzlaqltzVs_bwSFjYZvvDP5ub4uxqax

Volunteer Management Best Practices from a Seasoned Volunteer. (2026, January 23). Boardable.

https://boardable.com/resources/volunteer-management-best-practices-insights-from-an-experienced-volunteer/

Week, A. (2024, April 30). *Empowering Creative Teams: Strategies for ownership and accountability.* https://advertisingweek.com/empowering-creative-teams-strategies-for-ownership-and-accountability/

www.ingramcontent.com/pod-product-compliance
Lightning Source LLC
Chambersburg PA
CBHW071444130726
47997CB00006B/2221